THAI
in a week

D1742550

Somsong Buasai and David Smyth

Series Editors
Shirley Baldwin and Sarah Boas

ASIA BOOKS

ACKNOWLEDGMENTS

The authors and publishers are grateful to the following for supplying photographs:

APA Bangkok Guide: p. 67 (left)
Helen Brown: p. 42 (top)
Golden Tulip Hotel: p. 61
Robert Harding Picture Library: p. 47
Rachel Harrison: pp. 5, 10, 11, 13, 14 (top), 18, 23, 25, 28, 36, 54, 55, 56, 60, 65, 66, 70, 74 (bottom), 76 (bottom)
Office of the Information Attaché, Royal Thai Embassy: pp. 67 (right), 78
Dr. Michael Parnwell: pp. 14 (bottom), 16, 27, 34, 45, 51, 57, 76 (top)
THAI Airways International: pp. 4, 81
The Thai Red Cross Society: p. 74 (top)
Tourism Authority of Thailand: pp. 20, 39, 41 42 (bottom)

British Library Cataloguing in Publication Data
Buasai, Somsong
   Thai in a week.
   1. Spoken Thai language
   I. Title   II. Smyth, David *1954–*
   495.91342

   ISBN 0 340 52712 9

Thai in a Week
Published and distributed by:
Asia Books Co. Ltd.
5 Sukhumvit Soi 61, Sukhumvit Road
P.O. Box 11–40
Bangkok 10110, Thailand.
Tel: 3912680, 3910590
Fax: (662) 38 11 621

First published in the U.K. by Hodder and Stoughton Ltd.

© 1990 Somsong Buasai and David Smyth

Typeset by Wearside Tradespools, Fulwell, Sunderland
Printed in Hong Kong by Colorcraft Ltd.

CONTENTS

Thai in a week is a short course which will equip you to deal with everyday situations when you visit Thailand: asking for directions, taking taxis, shopping and so on.

The course is divided into 7 units, each corresponding to a day in the life of Jill and Frank, a young English couple visiting Thailand for the first time. Each unit is based on a dialogue which introduces the essential language items in a realistic context. Key phrases are highlighted in the dialogues and, as an additional aid, a line-by-line English translation is provided.

The dialogues are preceded by a brief 'cultural introduction' (look for this symbol: ▶ ▶ ▶) and each unit also includes a phrasebook section, short grammatical explanations and follow-up activities aimed at providing the basis for a more thorough understanding of the way the language works. Answers can be checked in a Key at the back of the book. English–Thai vocabulary is listed under topic headings on pp. 84–87 and is followed by a Thai–English vocabulary list.

Romanisation of Thai

เธอเล่าว่าต้องฝึกเช่นเดียวกับทหารอื่น ๆ ไม่ว่า
จะเป็นการเดินป่าโดดร่มส่งสัมภาระและอื่น ๆ
แต่ยังไม่เคยออกสนามรบจริง ๆ เพื่อนหญิงร่วม
งานของเธอมีทั้งสิ้น ๕๐ คน แต่ที่โดดร่มได้
มีเพียงไม่กี่คนเท่านั้น

An example of Thai script

Thai is written in its own unique script. While it is convenient to represent the language in romanised form for westerners wanting to learn it, it is important to realise that the romanised form is no more than a learning aid; it is not an acceptable alternative to the Thai script, and most Thais would not be able to understand it. It should also be pointed out that the romanisation system can only offer an approximate representation of Thai sounds. Wherever possible try to learn from the way you hear a word or sentence spoken, rather than trying to memorise pronunciations from the romanised spelling.

INTRODUCTION

PRONUNCIATION GUIDE

Thai is a **tonal** language. This means that the way you pronounce a syllable in Thai affects its meaning; for example, **see** means 'four' when pronounced with a *low tone* – that is, with the voice pitched slightly lower than normal – and 'colour' if it is said with a *rising* tone – similar to a questioning intonation in English. While learning to both hear and produce the correct tone is important, don't let a fear of getting a tone wrong inhibit you from practising Thai. In the past, travel writers have greatly exaggerated the difficulty of tones with tall stories about tonal *faux pas* that have transformed polite remarks into shocking obscenities. Wrong tones are very seldom the cause of misunderstanding or communication breakdowns, and there are certainly many westerners who manage to operate confidently and effectively with much less than perfect accuracy in their tones.

Tones

There are five tones in Thai: the mid tone, low tone, high tone, rising tone and falling tone. The following symbols are used to represent the tones in the romanisation system: mid tone (*no mark*); low tone (`` ` ``); high tone (´); rising tone (ˇ); falling tone (ˆ). At the beginning of the tape you will hear a Thai speaker reading the words below, to illustrate how the different tones sound. Listen carefully and try to imitate the speaker's pronunciation. Don't worry about what the words mean at this stage!

mid tone:	mah	bpai	nahn	kOOn	rohng rairm
	pairng	dee	gin	dairng	wun
low tone:	yàhng	bài	sìp	gùp	yòo
	pèt	yàhk	fàhk	yài	sài
high tone:	róo	lék	láir-o	krúp	kít
	nórng	rót	púk	cháo	náhm
rising tone:	săhm	năi	wăhn	kŏr	yĭng
	sĕe-a	lŭng	dĕe-o	sŏrng	pŏm
falling tone:	mâi	châi	dâi	hâi	têe
	hâh	mâhk	pôot	chôrp	dtôrng

Consonants

At the beginning of a word, the consonants are pronounced similarly to the way they would be in English. The following sounds however need further clarification:

g   as in *get* (and not *gin*)

1

ng   This sound only occurs at the end of words in English, like 'sing', 'wrong', 'king' etc. On the tape you can hear a Thai saying the following words beginning with **ng**. Listen and try to imitate the sound:

ngahn   ngún   ngai   ngoo   ngahm

bp   This sound is somewhere between a *b* sound in English and a *p* sound. Don't be discouraged if you can't produce it at first; it often takes even the most committed learners of the language some time before they can hear the difference between **b** and **bp** and produce it. Here are some examples of common Thai words beginning with this sound that you can hear on the tape:

bpai   bplào   bpra-tâyt   bpoo   bpàhk

dt   This sound is somewhere between a *t* sound in English and a *d* sound, and like **bp** often causes a few problems at the beginning. Again, don't be discouraged if you can't produce it immediately. Listen to these words on the tape and try to imitate them:

dtìt   dtahm   dtôrng   dtòr   dtee

k, p, t   When the sounds **k**, **p**, and **t** occur at the end of words, for example in words like **mâhk, chôrp**, and **bàht**, they sound different from English words ending in the same sounds. This is because the final consonant sound is not *released* even though the mouth is positioned to make that sound. Listen to a Thai on the tape saying these groups of three words. At first you will probably think they sound identical but very quickly you will find you are able to distinguish between them quite easily.

bàhk	bàhp	bàht		rêek	rêep	rêet
lôok	lôop	lôot		yàhk	yàhp	yàht

Vowels

Most Thai vowels and vowel sounds are fairly straightforward and have near equivalents in English:

a as in *ago*
e as in *pen*
i as in *bit*
o as in *cot*
u as in *fun*

ah as in *father*	**er** as in *number*
ai as in *Thai*	**ew** as in *few*
air as in *fair*	**oh** as in *go*
ao as in *Laos*	**oo** as in *boot*
ay as in *may*	**OO** as in *book*
ee as in *fee*	**oy** as in *boy*

More tricky sounds which are difficult to compare with the sounds of English are recorded on the tape. Listen and try to imitate the speaker's pronunciation:

eu	meu	keu	séu	rĕu
eu-a	mêu-a	reu-a	sêu-a	néu-a
air-o	láir-o	gâir-o	tăir-o	mair-o
er-ee	ler-ee	ker-ee	ner-ee	chĕr-ee

*(Note: the **r** in **er-ee** is silent)*

Some peculiarities of colloquial Thai

Many Thais are unable to produce a clear **r** sound at the beginning of a syllable and substitute an **l** sound instead. Thus you will commonly hear **a-lai na?** 'Pardon?' instead of **a-rai na?** You might also hear Thais omit the second consonant sound at the beginning of words, so that **krúp** becomes **kúp** and **bprêe-o** becomes **bpêe-o**; and don't be too surprised if you hear **făh** for **kwăh** (right) since **f** is substituted by some speakers for **kw**!

Some major differences between Thai and English

Apart from its tones, Thai differs from English and other more familiar western languages in many other ways. With neither complicated verb tenses nor singular and plural forms of nouns to memorise some people erroneously conclude that Thai has no grammar. All languages have grammar, although not all languages have the same grammatical priorities and distinctions. In the case of Thai, for example, there are many more words for 'you' than in European languages, the particular choice of word taking into account the age, relationship and relative status between speakers. Then Thai has *particles*, untranslateable words that are tagged onto the end of sentences, sometimes to convey a polite tone and sometimes to serve a grammatical function, such as changing a sentence into a command. If you study the Thai sentences carefully, you will soon notice that there is often no word-for-word correspondence between Thai and English. Frequently Thai completely omits pronouns, or uses three verbs where English has one, or uses a verb where English uses a noun. The Thai-English vocabulary at the back of the book will enable you to look more closely at the way the Thai sentences in the dialogues are constructed.

Some remarks on Thai culture

You will find that your attempt, no matter how modest, to learn a little Thai, will be warmly received by Thais, especially outside Bangkok. It is also worth going to the trouble of learning a little bit about Thai culture and patterns of behaviour: about the importance of showing consideration, especially to older people; about the importance of a *cool heart* – not losing your temper – and avoiding confrontations that can result in another's loss of face; about the position of the monarchy and Buddhism in Thai society; about Thai body language, such as not pointing with your feet or sitting with your feet stretched out in front of you and not touching people on the head. A little background reading will greatly enhance your enjoyment of your visit.

ASKING WHERE THINGS ARE

▶ ▶ **Arrival** When you arrive at Don Muang airport you will find customs and passport procedures easy to follow. Notices are in English and staff and officials will all speak English; they do not expect foreigners to be able to speak Thai. Hotel rooms and fixed-rate taxis can be booked at the appropriate counters in the airport foyer; money can also be changed here. Again, staff manning these counters will be able to speak English, and since they are likely to be busy, it is advisable to carry out these transactions in English, unless you are very fluent in Thai.

The first time that most visitors need to speak Thai is when they want to ask where somewhere or something is.

rohng rairm yòo têe-nǎi?/where's the hotel?

Frank and Jill, a young English couple on holiday in Thailand, have been sightseeing near their hotel in central Bangkok. They've got a bit lost and Frank decides to try out his Thai on a passer-by:

Frank: **kǒr-tôht** krúp   rohng rairm ree-yen **yòo têe-nǎi?**
            ***Excuse me. Where's** the Regent Hotel?*

Passer-by: rohng rairm ree-yen lěr?   **yòo têe-nôhn**
            *The Regent Hotel? **It's over there.***

Frank: glai mái krúp?
            Is it far?

Passer-by: mâi glai krúp
            No, it isn't.

Frank: **kòrp-kOOn mâhk** krúp
            Thank you very much.

Passer-by: mâi bpen rai
            That's all right.

hôrng náhm yòo têe-nǎi?/where's the toilet?

Later that day, Frank and Jill are in a restaurant. They want to know where the toilet is.

Frank: **kǒr-tôht** krúp   hôrng
náhm **yòo têe-nǎi?**
*Excuse me. Where's
the toilet?*

Waitress: **yòo** têe-nôhn
kâ   hôrng náhm pôo-
chai **yòo** tahng
kwǎh   hôrng náhm
pôo-yǐng **yòo** tahng sái
*It's over there. The
men's is on the right.
The ladies' is on the
left.*

ญ

หญิง

Ladies' toilet

Frank: **kòrp-kOOn krúp**
Thank you.

ช

Waitress: kâ
That's O.K.

ชาย

Men's toilet

bpai . . . séu dtǒo-a têe-nǎi?/
where do I buy a ticket for . . . ?

At the Northern Bus Station Jill and Frank are wondering where they should buy tickets for Chiangmai.

Jill: kǒr-tôht kâ   bpai chee-ung mài **séu dtǒo-a têe-nǎi?**
*Excuse me. **Where do you buy tickets** for Chiangmai?*

Clerk: séu têe-nêe krúp
You buy them here.

Jill: kòrp-kOOn kâ   láir-o **kêun rót may têe-nǎi** ká?
*Thank you. And **where do you get on the bus**?*

Clerk: têe-nôhn krúp
Over there.

Jill: kòrp-kOOn mâhk kâ
Thank you very much.

Clerk: mâi bpen rai krúp
Not at all.

USEFUL WORDS AND PHRASES

kǒr-tôht krúp/kâ	Excuse me/Sorry
. . . yòo têe-nǎi?	Where's . . . ?
hôrng náhm	toilet
rohng rairm	hotel
sa-tǎh-nee rót may	bus station
bprai-sa-nee	post office
. . . yòo glai mái?	Is . . . far?
glai mái?	Is it far?
yòo têe-nêe	It's here/Here it is
yòo têe-nôhn	It's over there/There it is
(yòo) glai	It's a long way
(yòo) mâi glai	It's not far
yòo tahng kwǎh	It's on the right
yòo tahng sái	It's on the left
kòrp-kOOn (mâhk) krúp/kâ	Thank you (very much)
mâi bpen rai krúp/kâ	That's all right/Not at all
dtǒo-a	ticket
rót may	bus
bpai . . . séu dtǒo-a têe-nǎi?	Where do you buy tickets to go to . . . ?
bpai . . . jorng dtǒo-a têe-nǎi?	Where do you book tickets to go to . . . ?
bpai . . . kêun rót may têe-nǎi?	Where do you get on the bus to go to . . . ?

the way it works

Being polite (krúp/kâ)

An important way of making your speech sound polite in Thai, is to add a 'polite'
particle – for which there is no exact English translation – at the end of statements
and questions. Male speakers say **krúp** at the end of both questions and statements,
while female speakers say **ká** at the end of a question and **kâ** at the end of a
statement. Thais use these particles when talking to strangers, people of senior
status, and in formal situations. For the foreigner, at first, it is probably best to use
polite particles when talking to any adult, and risk sounding too polite. When you
are more familiar with the language you will see when and with whom you can omit
polite particles without appearing rude. **krúp** and **kâ** can also be used on their own
as a response, meaning, 'Yes', 'Right' or 'O.K.'

mâi bpen rai

mâi bpen rai is how you should respond if someone thanks you. It can be translated
as 'That's all right', 'It's a pleasure' or by any other standard response to thanks. It
can also mean 'It doesn't matter', 'Never mind', 'Don't worry about it', so it is also an
appropriate response to apologies and excuses.

Asking questions

In Thai, the question word usually comes at the end of the sentence:

hôrng náhm	yòo	têe-nǎi?	Where's the toilet?
toilet	is situated	*where?*	

bprai-sa-nee	**lěr?**	The post office?
post office	*(question word)*?	
glai	**mái?**	Is it far?
far	*(question word)*?	

There are no equivalent words in English for the question words **lěr?** and **mái?** The former is conveyed by a rising intonation in English and the latter by inverting the order of the subject and verb.

Answering questions

To answer 'Where . . . ?' questions, the word **têe-nǎi?** is replaced by the answer:

hôrng náhm	**yòo**	**têe-nǎi?**	Where's the toilet?
(**hôrng náhm**)	**yòo**	**têe-nôhn**	(The toilet is) It's over there.
	yòo	**têe-nêe**	It's here.
	yòo	**tahng kwǎh**	It's on the right.
	yòo	**tahng sái**	It's on the left.

(Notice that there is no need to use a Thai equivalent for 'it')

mái? questions demand yes – no answers. To say 'yes', you simply repeat the verb:

glai mái?	Is it far?
glai	Yes.
bpai mái?	Are (you) going?
bpai	Yes.
séu mái?	Are (you) buying (it)?
séu	Yes.

To say 'no', you use the negative word ***mâi*** in front of the verb:

glai mái?	Is it far?
mâi glai	No.
bpai mái?	Are (you) going?
mâi bpai	No.
séu mái?	Are (you) buying (it)?
mâi séu	No.

Make sure that you don't confuse the question word **mái?** which occurs at the end of a sentence, with the negative word **mâi** which occurs in front of verbs!

Verbs

Unlike verbs in western languages Thai verbs have a single fixed form which does not change to match the subject or the tense. Sometimes a specific word is added in front of or after the verb to indicate when the action took place (we shall meet some of these later in the book). Often, however, the context offers the only clue as to whether the verb is referring to the present, past or future. For the westerner this can be confusing at first; for Thais, of course, it is perfectly straightforward and does not lead to the kind of misunderstandings and missed appointments that the westerner imagines!

Some useful Thai verbs:

to buy	**séu**	to ask (a question)	**tǎhm**	to eat/drink	**gin**
to book	**jorng**	to speak	**pôot**	to come	**mah**
to go	**bpai**				

7

Pronouns

Thai has a more complex set of pronouns than English; there are different words for 'I' depending on whether the speaker is male (**pǒm**) or female (**chún, dee-chún**) and several different words for 'you', the appropriate choice depending on the ages of the speakers, their relationship and their relative status. In fact, the westerner can get along quite adequately with only a small number of pronouns which we shall meet as we go along. (You will also find a list of pronouns in the English–Thai topic vocabulary on p. 87.)

Another unusual aspect of Thai pronouns is that they are often omitted. As a result, it is sometimes difficult, when listening to Thais, to know who or what exactly is being spoken about! **séu** can, for example, mean I/you/he/we, etc. buy/bought/will buy, etc. Again Thais find this quite natural and totally unambiguous and, with practice, you will find that the ambiguities begin to disappear.

Adjectives

Adjectives in Thai follow the noun they refer to:

rót sǒo-ay   a/the beautiful car
(car beautiful)

Thai does not use the verb 'to be' with adjectives so most adjectives also function as verbs. (In the examples of questions the word **glai** (far) is referred to as a verb.)

glai   far/to be far
sǒo-ay   beautiful/to be beautiful

Thus **rót sǒo-ay** can be translated either as 'a beautiful car' or 'the car is beautiful'.

Nouns

Thai nouns do not have separate forms for singular and plural. To the western learner, this again seems bound to cause all kinds of ambiguity; in fact, when it is necessary to make a very clear distinction which would not be apparent from the context of the conversation, Thai adds certain 'pluralizer' words.

things to do

1.1   You are sightseeing in Bangkok. Stop a passer-by and ask where the following places are: (the first one is done for you)
      1   Regent Hotel (**rohng rairm ree-yen**)   **kǒr-tôht krúp/kâ   rohng-rairm ree-yen yòo têe-nǎi?**
      2   Lido Cinema (**rohng nǔng lee-doh**)
      3   Central Department Store (**hâhng sen-trun**)
      4   Temple of the Emerald Buddha (**wút prá-gâir-o**)
      Don't forget to use **krúp/kâ** as appropriate. You can find further help with asking directions later.

1.2   You are at the Northern Bus Station in Bangkok; how would you ask
       where . . .
       1   to book a ticket to Chiangmai (**chee-ung mài**)?
       2   to buy a ticket to Chiangrai (**chee-ung rai**)?
       3   to get on a bus for Lampang (**lum-bpahng**)?

1.3   Frank and Jill return to their hotel room to find that their bags (**gra-bpăo**)
       have disappeared (**hăi**). Listen to the dialogue on the tape and see if you
       can understand what is being said. The Thai text appears with a
       translation in the Key on p. 82.

TAKING A TAXI

Transport in Bangkok   You can travel around Bangkok by ordinary bus, air-conditioned bus, taxi or *samlor* (**săhm-lór**), the three-wheeled motorized pedi-cab, also known as a **dtÓOk-dtÓOk**. Street-maps indicating bus routes are widely available in bookshops and hotels and are an invaluable aid, both for the budget-conscious traveller, and for getting your bearings. The city's thousands of air-conditioned taxis provide a convenient and relatively cheap alternative to the public transport system. There are no taxi ranks, but with so many taxis and *samlors* on the road, finding one is seldom a problem. To call a taxi, you should raise your hand and signal to the driver with a beckoning motion, with the fingers pointing *downwards*.

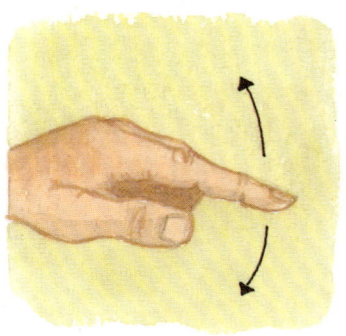

It is a good idea to check first that the driver knows the place you want to get to; then agree the price *before* you step into the vehicle. It is customary to haggle *a little* over the price, but in a relaxed and easy-going manner. Try to find out from a Thai beforehand what a reasonable price for the journey you plan would be, and if you find you have to pay a little more, accept the fact gracefully, and think of the journey as the opportunity for a cheap Thai lesson! You pay for your journey when you have reached your destination. Tipping is not customary; exceptions to this might be hotel limousine services or occasions when a particularly nasty traffic jam seriously increases the length of time your journey takes.

bpai . . . tâo-rài?/How much to go to . . . ?

Jill and Frank have been out shopping and want to take a taxi back to their hotel.

Frank: **róo-jùk** rohng rairm ree-yen **mái?**
Do you know the Regent Hotel?

Taxi: róo-jùk krúp
Yes.

Frank: **bpai tâo-rài?**
How much (will you charge)?

Taxi: jèt-sìp bàht krúp
70 baht.

Frank: jèt-sìp bàht lěr krúp? pairng **bpai nòy**
70 baht? That's a bit expensive.

Taxi: **mâi** pairng **ròrk** krúp rót dtìt mâhk
No, it's not expensive at all. The traffic is jammed.

Frank: **hâh-sìp bàht** dâi **mái?**
How about 50 baht?

Taxi: mâi dâi krúp hòk-sìp bàht gôr láir-o gun
No, I can't. I'll settle for 60 baht.

Frank: oh kay hòk-sìp bàht ná
O.K. 60 baht, right?

USEFUL WORDS AND PHRASES

táirk-sêe	taxi
săhm-lór	samlor
dtÓOk-dtÓOk	'tuk-tuk'
róo-jùk . . . mái?	Do you know . . . ?
bpai . . . tâo-rài?	How much to go to . . . ?
pairng	expensive
tòok	cheap

pairng bpai nòy	That's a little expensive
glai	far
glâi	near
. . . bàht dâi mái?	Can you go for . . . baht?
lée-o sái	Turn left
lée-o kwăh	Turn right
ler-ee bpai èek	Go straight on
ler-ee bpai èek nít nèung	Go on a bit further
jòrt . . .	Park/pull up . . .
. . . têe-nôhn	. . . over there
. . . dtrong née	. . . just here
mâi pairng ròrk	It's not expensive
rót dtìt	traffic jam/the traffic is jammed
. . . bàht gôr láir-o gun	(*idiomatic expression used in bargaining indicating last offer*) I/We'll settle for . . . baht

glai (far) and *glâi* (near)   To the westerner it seems particularly perverse that two words with exactly opposite meanings should sound almost the same. To the Thai of course, they don't sound the same at all. If you find your ears are not to be relied upon when it comes to distinguishing tones, it can save you some expensive taxi rides if you remember that the one you hear reduplicated (i.e. spoken *twice*) is usually 'near' (*glâi glâi*)!

the way it works

How much?

The question word **tâo-rài?** ('how much?') also appears at the end of the sentence:

bpai	**rohng rairm ree-yen**	**tâo-rài?**	How much is it to the Regent Hotel?
go	Regent Hotel	*how much?*	

In full-sentence answers to **tâo-rài?** questions, the number also appears at the end of the sentence (**séu dtŏo-a bpai chee-ung mài sŏrng róy bàht** He bought a ticket for Chiangmai for 200 baht) but in normal speech people tend to respond in shortened form.

Negative sentences

Negative sentences are formed by putting the word **mâi** in front of the main verb.

pŏm (chún) mâi bpai   I'm not going

Remember that words for 'expensive', 'far', 'good', 'tasty', etc. which in English we think of as adjectives, are regarded as both adjectives and verbs in Thai. Thus **mâi pairng** can be translated into English as 'It's not expensive' or simply as 'No', if it is the answer to a question **pairng mái?** (Is it expensive?)

When **mâi** occurs with **ròrk** in sentences like **mâi pairng ròrk** and **mâi glai ròrk**, the word **ròrk** conveys the idea of the speaker contradicting what has been said (or even thought) before. Thus, **pŏm mâi bpai ròrk** means 'I'm not going' (contrary to what you may have thought); in English we sometimes use '. . . at all' to convey this sense of contradiction.

Can (dâi)

The Thai word for 'can' is **dâi**. The important thing to remember is that it comes at the end of the sentence, after the main verb:

séu dtǒo-a bpai chee-ung mài *dâi* (You) *can* buy a ticket for Chiangmai.
bpai rohng nǔng lee-doh *dâi* **mái?** *Can* (we) go to the Lido Cinema?

(*Note that there are no pronouns in the Thai examples, and those supplied in brackets in the English translation, could just as well have been 'I', 'she' or 'they'*)

Questions that end in . . . **dâi mái?** (Can . . . ?) are answered either **dâi** (yes) or **mâi dâi** (no).

ná

ná is a particle which you will hear Thais use all the time but for which there is no single adequate English translation. It takes time to feel confident about using such words, but you can begin to get a feel for them by memorising short phrases when they occur in the dialogues. (You can find an example in Frank's conversation with the taxi-driver on p. 11.)

things to do

1.4 You want to get a taxi. How would you signal to the driver to stop? How would you ask the fare to the following places?

1 Regent Hotel
2 Siam Square (**sa-yǎhm sa-kwair**)
3 the airport (**sa-nǎhm bin**)
4 Sanam Luang (**sa-nǎhm lǒo-ung**)

1.5 The taxi-driver tells you the fare. What is the fare he quotes? Tell him that the price he suggests is a little expensive and offer him 20 baht less. (You can check numbers in the English-Thai topic vocabularies on p. 84.) Again the first example has been done for you.

1 Taxi-driver: jèt-sìp bàht krúp
   You: **pairng bpai nòy krúp/kâ   hâh-sìp bàht dâi mái?**
2 gâo-sìp bàht krúp
3 bpàirt-sìp bàht krúp
4 sǒrng-róy-jèt-sìp bàht krúp
5 hòk-sìp bàht krúp

1.6 How would you tell a taxi-driver to stop . . .
1 just here?   3 on the right?
2 over there?   4 on the left?

BUYING A DRINK

Refreshment   Thailand is always hot, so until you become used to the heat you will probably need to make frequent stops for refreshment. Fortunately there is no shortage of places selling cold drinks, ranging from road-side vendors to air-conditioned coffee shops, complete with menus in English and English-speaking waiters or waitresses. In the ordinary noodle shops found in almost every street, it is less likely that English will be understood. Wherever you choose to stop, the rule is to sit down and wait to be served and pay when you are ready to go, leaving a small tip in air-conditioned premises, but not in ordinary noodle shops. If you have difficulty attracting a waiter's attention, you can raise your hand and beckon with your fingers pointed *downwards* (just as when calling a taxi). You can also call out, **kOOn krúp/ká** (literally 'you') if the waiter or waitress is an adult, or **nǒo nǒo** (literally 'little mouse' – an affectionate way of addressing young children) if he or she is still a child.

têe ráhn gǒo-ay dtěe-o/in a noodle shop

After a couple of hours sightseeing in the heat, Jill and Frank decide to go into a noodle shop to get a cool drink and rest for a while.

14

Girl: ao **a-rai** ká?
       What would you like?

Frank: **kǒr koh-lâh kòo-ut nèung**
       Could I have a bottle of Coke?

Girl: koh-lâh mâi yen kâ   bpép-sêe dâi mái?
       The Coke's not cold. Will Pepsi do?

Frank: dâi   láir-o ao núm ma-práo gâir-o nèung dôo-ay
       Yes. And I'd like a glass of coconut juice, too.

Girl: núm ma-práo mâi mee kâ   **mee** bpép-sêe koh-lâh fairn-dtâh
       láir-o gôr bee-a
       *We haven't got any coconut juice. **There's** Pepsi, Coke, Fanta*
       and beer.

Frank: **ao bpép-sêe sǒrng kòo-ut** gôr láir-ɔ gun
       We'll have two Pepsis then.

When you are ready to pay, you can say either **gèp dtung na** (literally
'Collect the money') or **kǒr bin nòy** (Can I have the bill please?). The latter
is more appropriate in expensive restaurants and coffee shops.

Drinks

bee-a	beer
bee-a sǐng	*Singha* beer
núm chah	tea
chah dum yen	iced black tea
gah-fair	coffee
gah-fair yen	iced coffee
oh-lée-ung	iced black coffee
núm ma-práo	coconut juice
núm sôm	orange juice
núm sôm kún	fresh orange juice
núm ma-nao	lime juice
mâir-kǒhng	*Mekhong* (local whisky)
koh-lâh	Coke
bpép-sêe	Pepsi
green sa-bpòrt	Green Spot (a popular fizzy orange drink)
fairn-dtâh	Fanta
núm soh-dah	soda water
náhm	water
núm kǎirng bplào gâir-o nèung	a glass of water

USEFUL WORDS AND PHRASES

ráhn gǒo-ay dtěe-o	noodle shop
kòo-ut	bottle
gâir-o	glass
tôo-ay	cup
kOOn krúp (ká)/nǒo nǒo	waiter/waitress!
ao a-rai?	What would you like?
kǒr . . .	Can I have . . . ? I'd like . . .
ao . . .	want; I want, I'll have . . .
yen	cool, cold
rórn	hot
hěw náhm	thirsty
kǒr/ao . . . kòo-ut nèung	I'd like a bottle of . . .
kǒr/ao . . . tôo-ay nèung	I'd like a cup of . . .
kǒr/ao . . . gâir-o nèung	I'd like a glass of . . .
kǒr/ao . . . sǒrng kòo-ut	We'd like two bottles of . . .
láir-o gôr	and/and then
dôo-ay	too
gèp dtung/kǒr bin nòy	Can I have the bill?

the way it works

Ordering drinks

When you want to order something in a restaurant or coffee shop you can use either **kǒr** or **ao** to mean 'I'd like' or 'we'd like'. Notice that there is no Thai word for 'please'. Normally, politeness is conveyed both in the choice of words (**kǒr**, for example, is a polite way of asking for something) and by the use of particles **krúp/kâ**. When ordering food and drinks in restaurants or coffee shops these particles can be safely omitted without causing offence or appearing rude.

Numbers and counting

In English, *uncountable nouns*, like butter, bread, sand and cement can only be counted by the container in which they are stored or purchased. In Thai *every* noun is uncountable: if you want to quantify a noun you have to use a special word called a *classifier* with that noun. The classifiers for nouns in this unit have exact equivalents in English but the classifiers for certain items that are countable in English, such as bananas or chairs cannot be readily translated. (A list of the most common classifiers is given in the English–Thai topic vocabularies on p. 87.) Look at the examples below. Notice that if the number is *one* it comes after the classifier, but if it is *more than one*, it comes before the classifier.

koh-lâh *kòo-ut* nèung	one *bottle* of Coke
koh-lâh sŏrng *kòo-ut*	two *bottles* of Coke
gah-fair *tôo-ay* nèung	one *cup* of coffee
gah-fair săhm *tôo-ay*	three *cups* of coffee
núm sôm *gâir-o* nèung	one *glass* of orange juice
núm sôm sèe *gâir-o*	four *glasses* of orange juice

things to do

.1 How would you order the following:
1 a bottle of *Singha* beer?
2 a glass of water?
3 three bottles of Coke?
4 two cups of coffee?
5 five glasses of fresh orange juice?

.2 Can you match up the following orders with the right drinks?
1 koh-lâh hâh kòo-ut
2 núm sôm kún sèe gâir-o
3 bee-a sǐng sǎhm kòo-ut
4 núm kǎirng bplào sŏrng gâir-o
5 gah-fair sŏrng tôo-ay

  a   b   c   d   e

.3 You've gone to a noodle shop with three friends. Between you, you want two bottles of Pepsi, a glass of fresh orange juice and a cup of coffee. Can you call the waitress (a young girl) and order the drinks?

17

AT THE MARKET

▶ ▶ **Markets**   With their exotic fruits and mixture of pungent and mouth-watering smells Thai markets are fascinating places and well worth a visit. Smaller markets sell only fresh foodstuffs, household goods and cheap toiletries and usually close down in the early afternoon. The best time to go is at about 7 a.m. when there is lots of activity, with housewives and maids haggling noisily as they go about the day's shopping. It is particularly interesting to browse around the huge weekend market at Chatuchak Park (**sǒo-un jùt-dtÒO-jùk**) where a much wider range of goods are on sale: furniture, pets, material and clothing, electrical goods, crockery, 'antiques', plants, books, tapes – just about everything in fact. Markets are also good places for trying out your Thai.

séu pǒn-la-mái/buying fruit

Wandering around a market near their hotel, Jill and Frank stop to buy some fruit.

Jill: **sôm loh la tâo-rài?**
   How much a kilo are the oranges?
Vendor: săhm-sìp bàht kâ
   30 baht.

Jill: sǎhm-sìp lěr?   pairng ná
30? That's expensive.

Vendor: mâi pairng ròrk kâ   **a-ròy kâ**   wǎhn ná   lorng chim doo nòy
si ká   **a-ròy mái?**
*No it's not. **They're tasty.** They're (nice and) sweet. Try some.*
Does it taste nice?

Jill: **a-ròy**   yêe-sìp-hâh dâi mái?
***Yes.** How about 25 baht?*

Vendor: yêe-sìp-jèt gôr láir-o gun   ao **gèe** loh ká?
*I'll settle for 27. **How many** kilos do you want?*

Jill: ao loh dee-o
I want just one.

Next to the oranges are some unfamiliar looking fruits resembling
oak-apples. Frank is intrigued . . .

Frank: **nêe a-rai krúp?**
What are these?

Vendor: lum-yai kâ
They're lamyai (longan).

Frank: **a-rai ná?**
Pardon?

Vendor: rêe-uk wâh lum-yai kâ
They're called 'lamyai'.

Frank: lum-yai **châi mái?**
*'Lamyai', **is that right?***

Vendor: **châi** kâ   tòok láir-o
***Yes.** That's right.*

Frank: **loh la tâo-rài?**
How much are they per kilo?

Vendor: **loh la** sǎhm-sìp-hâh kâ
*35 baht **per kilo**.*

Frank: lót nòy dâi mái?
Can you lower it a bit?

Vendor: sǒrng loh hòk-sìp-hâh gôr láir-o gun
I'll let you have two kilos for 65 baht.

USEFUL WORDS AND PHRASES

dta-làht	market
pǒn-la-mái	fruit
. . . loh la tâo-rài?	How much a kilo are . . . ?
ao loh dee-o	I want just one kilo
ao sǒrng loh	I want two kilos
lót nòy dâi mái?	Can you lower the price a bit?
lorng chim doo nòy si	Go on, try one/a bit
a-ròy ná	It's/They're tasty
a-ròy mái?	Does it/Do they taste nice?
ao gèe loh?	How many kilos do you want?
nêe a-rai?	What is this/are these?
nêe rêe-uk wâh a-rai?	What is this/are these called?
pah-sǎh tai nêe rêe-uk wâh a-rai?	What is this/are these called in Thai?
a-rai ná?	Pardon?
rêe-uk wâh . . . châi mái?	It's/They're called . . . , is that right?

You will find a list of fruits in the English–Thai topic vocabularies on p. 86.

the way it works

. . . *per kilo* (loh la . . .)

Notice that the word order in Thai sentences where you want to use 'a' or 'per' is different from English:

sôm	**loh**	*la*	**tâo-rài?**	How much a kilo are oranges?
oranges	kilo	*per*	how much?	
(sôm)	**loh**	*la*	**sǎhm-sìp bàht**	(Oranges are) 30 baht a kilo.
(oranges)	kilo	*per*	30 baht	

Not all fruits are bought by the kilo; bananas are bought by the bunch (**wĕe**), while pineapples, papaya, mangoes and other larger fruit are bought individually, using the word **bai** in place of **loh**. The words **wĕe**, **bai** and **loh** are all classifiers.

glôo-ay	*wĕe*	la	tâo-rài?	How much are bananas per *bunch*?
	wĕe	la	săhm-sìp bàht	30 baht per *bunch*.
ma-la-gor	*bai*	la	tâo-rài?	How much are papayas per *fruit*?
	bai	la	yêe-sìp bàht	20 baht each/per *fruit*.
ma-môo-ung	*bai*	la	tâo-rài?	How much are mangoes per *fruit*?
	bai	la	sìp-hâh bàht	15 baht each.
sùp-bpa-rót	*bai*	la	tâo-rài?	How much are pineapples per *fruit*?
	bai	la	yêe-sìp-hâh bàht	25 baht each.

How many?

The question word **gèe** means 'how many . . . ?' It is always followed by a classifier.

bee-a gèe *kòo-ut*?	How many *bottles* of beer?
sôm gèe *loh*?	How many *kilos* of oranges?
gah-fair gèe *tôo-ay*?	How many *cups* of coffee?

If the answer to a **gèe . . . ?** question is *two or more* remember that the number comes *before* the classifier (**ma-môo-ung sŏrng bai** *two mangoes*), but if the number is only *one*, then it comes *after* the classifier (**sôm loh dee-o** *a single kilo of oranges*).

Another question form (. . . châi mái?)

. . . **châi mái?** is tagged on to the end of a statement to turn it into a question; a rather clumsy general translation is, ' . . . isn't that right?' but it is really equivalent to the *tag* question in English sentences like, 'He's coming, *isn't he?*', 'You did, *didn't you?*', 'I should, *shouldn't I?*' It is very useful for checking that you have understood something, or that your pronunciation is correct. A 'yes' answer to a . . . **châi mái?** question is simply **châi**, and a 'no' answer, **mâi châi**.

. . . mái? or . . . châi mái?

. . . **mái?** questions do not anticipate that the answer will be one thing or another; they are simply asking for information. . . . **châi mái?** questions make an assumption about the answer and ask for confirmation that the assumption is correct.

pairng *mái?*	Is it expensive?	**pairng** *châi mái?*	It's expensive, isn't it?
pairng	Yes.	**châi**	Yes.
a-ròy *mái?*	Is it tasty?	**a-ròy** *châi mái?*	It's tasty, isn't it?
a-ròy	Yes.	**châi**	Yes.

things to do

2.4 How would you ask the price if you wanted to buy these fruits? Use the classifier given in brackets.

1 glôo-ay (wĕe)
  glôo-ay wĕe la tâo-rài?

2 sôm (loh)

3 lum-yai (loh)

4 ma-la-gor (bai)

2.5 These were the prices the owner of the fruit stall quoted. Check with her that you heard the price correctly and then ask if she can lower the price a little. The first example has been done for you.

1 Vendor: glôo-ay wĕe la yêe-sìp-hâh (bàht) kâ
   You: **wĕe la yêe-sìp-hâh châi mái?   lót nòy dâi mái?**

2 sôm loh la sèe-sìp kâ
3 lum-yai loh la săhm-sìp-hâh kâ
4 ma-la-gor bai la sìp-bpàirt kâ
(*Note that it is quite natural to omit the word* **bàht** *in this context.*)

2.6   1 How would you ask what these fruits are called?

2 What would you say if you didn't understand the answer the first time?

MAKING A TELEPHONE CALL

Telephone calls These are a daunting prospect in any foreign language. If you have to make an important call, such as confirming flight times, it is best to speak in English or ask a Thai to phone on your behalf. But even on occasions when you want to contact an English-speaking Thai, you may need to carry out the preliminary exchanges in Thai, such as identifying yourself and asking for that person. If there is no English-speaker available at the other end, don't try to be too ambitious; it is better to bring the call to a smart conclusion in simple, limited Thai, than to find half-way through a sentence that you don't know the Thai words you need to make your point!

Telephone calls can be made from public kiosks, hotels and shops displaying a phone in a prominent position on the counter. Long-distance calls are best made either from major hotels or, in Bangkok, from the Central Post Office, just off New Road.

kǒr pôot gùp . . . ?/could I speak to . . . ?

A Thai friend, Somchai, has told Frank to give him a call when he reaches Bangkok, so Frank tries his home number:

Frank: hallo   **têe-nôhn bâhn kOOn Sǒm-chai châi mái?**
         Hello. Is that Khun Somchai's house?
Maid: châi kâ
         Yes.

Frank:	**kǒr pôot gùp** kOOn Sǒm-chai **nòy dâi mái krúp?**
	Could I speak to Khun Somchai please?
Maid:	krai pôot ká?
	Who's speaking please?
Frank:	**pǒm** Frank **pôot krúp** bpen pêu-un kOOn Sǒm-chai
	This is Frank speaking. I'm a friend of Somchai's.
Maid:	ror dǐe-o ná ká . . . kOOn Sǒm-chai mâi yòo kâ
	Wait a minute . . . Khun Somchai isn't in.
Frank:	glùp **mêu-rai** krúp?
	***When** will he be back?*
Maid:	glùp dtorn yen kâ
	He'll be back in the evening.
Frank:	a-rai ná?
	Pardon?
Maid:	glùp dtorn yen kâ
	He'll be back in the evening.
Frank:	krúp kòrp-kOOn krúp **sa-wùt dee** krúp
	*Right. Thank you. **Goodbye**.*
Maid:	kâ sa-wùt dee kâ
	O.K. Goodbye.

Using the telephone

toh-ra-sùp	telephone
ber toh-ra-sùp	telephone number
pǒm (chún) yàhk ja toh-ra-sùp	I'd like to make a phone call
hallo	Hello
têe-nôhn . . . châi mái?	Is that . . . ?
kǒr pôot gùp . . . nòy dâi mái krúp/ká?	Could I speak to . . . please?
kǒr dtòr ber . . . ?	Can I have extension . . . ?
pǒm (chún) . . . pôot krúp/ká	This is . . . speaking

Understanding the reply

krai pôot krúp/ká?	Who's speaking?
ror děe-o ná	Wait a minute
săi mâi wâhng	The line's engaged
săi mâi dee	It's a bad line
a-rai ná?	Pardon?
kŏr-tôht toh ber pit	Sorry, wrong number
. . . mâi yòo	. . . isn't in
. . . bpai tÓO-rá	. . . has gone out
. . . yung mâi glùp	. . . isn't back yet
mee a-rai ja sùng mái?	Can I take a message?
ber toh-ra-sùp tâo-rài?	What's (your/his, etc.) telephone number?
prÔOng née toh mah mài	I'll ring back tomorrow/Ring back tomorrow
děe-o toh mah mài	I'll ring back in a minute/Ring back in a minute
sa-wùt dee krúp/kâ	Goodbye

USEFUL WORDS AND PHRASES

pŏm (chún) mâi kâo jai	I don't understand
pôot dung dung nòy	Could you speak louder, please?
chôo-ay pôot cháh cháh nòy dâi mái?	Could you speak more slowly please?
pôot	to speak
glùp	to return
mah	to come
bpen	to be
bpen pêu-un . . .	I'm a friend of . . .

the way it works

kOOn

kOOn is a polite title used in front of first names, rather like 'Mr', 'Mrs', 'Miss', etc. It is used both as a polite way of addressing people and for referring to them in their absence. When dealing with adults you should at first always add **kOOn** before their name: it is better to be considered too polite than disrespectful. **kOOn** is also the most common word for 'you'.

When?

The Thai word for 'when?' is **mêu-rai?** Like most Thai question words, it usually occurs at the end of the sentence.

kOOn Sŏm-chai glùp *mêu-rai?*	*When* does Khun Somchai return?
kOOn mah meu-ung tai *mêu-rai?*	*When* are you coming to Thailand?

Notice that there is no word to indicate tense in these examples; the first question might just as correctly have been translated as 'When *did* Khun Somchai return?' or 'When *will* Khun Somchai return?' Generally, it is perfectly clear from the context whether the past, present or future is being referred to.

Useful expressions of time

dtorn	a period of time
dtorn cháo	in the morning
dtorn bài	in the afternoon
dtorn yen	in the evening
dtorn glahng keun	in the night
dtorn glahng wun	in the daytime
děe-o	in a minute
wun	day
ah-tít	week
deu-un	month
bpee	year
wun née	today
prÔOng née	tomorrow
mêu-a wahn née	yesterday
nahn	a long time
ah-tít nâh	next week
èek sŏrng ah-tít	in two weeks' time

Past time can be expressed using the words **mêu-a . . . gòrn**:

mêu-a **săhm ah-tít** *gòrn*	three weeks *ago*
mêu-a **bpee** *gòrn*	*last* year
pŏm (chún) mah meu-ung tai *mêu-a* **sìp wun** *gòrn*	I came to Thailand ten days *ago*

The pronoun 'I'

There are numerous ways of saying 'I' in Thai. The most appropriate forms for foreigners are **pŏm** for male speakers and **dee-chún** or its abbreviated form, **chún**, for females. Frequently, however, as you know, the pronoun is completely omitted.

The verb 'to be'

The verb **bpen** can frequently be translated as 'is', 'are', 'am'. However, there are situations when it is incorrect to translate these English words using **bpen**. The most important thing to remember about **bpen** is that it must always be followed by a noun:

pŏm bpen *pêu-un* **kOOn Sŏm-chai**	I'm a *friend* of Somchai's.

And don't forget that **bpen** should *not* be used before an adjective to translate phrases like 'it is expensive' 'the hotel is near' 'the lamyai are delicious'. The Thai adjectives **pairng** (expensive), **glâi** (near) and **a-ròy** (delicious) are also the verbs 'to be expensive' 'to be near' and 'to be delicious'.

things to do

2.7a You want to ring various Thai friends to let them know you've arrived in Bangkok. How would you ask to speak to each of the friends listed in your diary? Don't forget to use **kOOn** before the first name and since you are ringing Chartchai at work, you will have to ask for his extension number.

Khun Malee (home) 583 0391
Khun Chartchai (work) 287 9541 ext. 356
Khun Surachai (home) 369 5288

2.7b Now listen to the cassette to hear the response on the other end of the line. How many of your friends could you get through to? (You can also find out what was said over the phone in the Key on p. 82.)

2.8 When you try to ring Noy, you get through to her secretary.
1   Secretary: Hallo!
    [Ask if you can speak to Noy]
2   Secretary: krai pôot ká?
    [Give your name and explain that you are a friend of Noy's]
3   Secretary: kOOn Nóy mâi yòo kâ mee a-rai ja sùng mái?
    [Say you will ring back in the afternoon. Thank her and say goodbye]

VISITING FRIENDS

กรุณากดกริ่ง

Ring the bell

ระวังสุนัขดุ

Beware of the dog

If you are invited to a Thai home, there are a few rules of Thai etiquette that should be observed. You should remove your shoes just before entering the house: there will usually be several pairs lying in front of the door which will remind you and show you where to put them. Once inside, members of the household may greet you with a **wâi** – a gesture of greeting and respect in which the hands are placed together in a prayer-like position in front of the face at approximately chin height. You should return this greeting. The height at which the hands are held reflects the degree of respect you wish to convey. Thus, adults will hold their hands so that the tips of their fingers are near their chins when responding to a child's *wai*, but nearer their forehead when greeting an older person. Another way in which Thais try to show respect for older people is by keeping their head at a lower level when passing by or talking to them. This does not have to be taken too literally: an obvious attempt to bend forward a little when passing a seated person, for example, is adequate and appreciated. (The head, incidentally, is a taboo area; *never* attempt to give a Thai a friendly pat on the head or ruffle his or her hair.) Finally, as a general rule, dress smartly and on the conservative side.

bpai yêe-um pêu-un/a social call

Frank and Jill call round at Somchai's house where they are greeted by Somchai's wife, Janya:

Janya: **sa-wùt dee** kâ kOOn Frank   kOOn Frank **sa-bai dee lěr** ká?
         Hello, Frank. *How are you?*

Frank: sa-bai dee krúp   **láir-o** kOOn Jun-yah **lâ** krúp?
         I'm fine. How about you, Janya?

Janya: sa-bai dee **měu-un gun** kâ
         *I'm fine, **too**.*

Frank: nêe Jill fairn pǒm
         This is my wife, Jill.

Janya: sa-wùt dee kâ kOOn Jill   chern kâhng nai ná ká   kOOn
         Sǒm-chai **yung mâi** glùp
         Hello Jill. Please come in. *Khun Somchai **isn't** back **yet**.*

pôot tai gèng/you speak Thai well

One of the most pleasant surprises for anyone attempting to learn Thai is the praise and encouragement that Thais so readily offer. Sometimes it takes less than half a dozen faltering words to prompt a complimentary **pôot tai gèng**. Such flattery is marvellous both for the ego and as an incentive to learn and practise more, but don't take it too literally. The paying of such compliments is an important aspect of Thai social relations. See how Janya makes Jill feel good about her linguistic skill:

Janya: kOOn Jill **pôot pah-sǎh tai bpen mái?**
         Can you speak Thai, Jill?

Jill: **pôot bpen** nít-nòy
         I can a bit.

Janya: or . . . **pôot tai gèng** ná   yòo meu-ung tai nahn mái?
         Oh you speak Thai well. Have you been in Thailand long?

Jill: mâi nahn kâ   sǒrng sǎhm wun **tâo-nún**
         *Not long. **Only** two or three days.*

Janya:	sŏrng săhm wun tâo-nún lĕr? măir! kOOn Jill pôot chút **jìng jìng**
	*Only two or three days? Goodness! You **really** speak clearly.*
Jill:	bplào kâ pôot dâi nít-nòy tâo-nún dtàir **yàhk ja** pôot dâi dee
	*No. I can only speak a little bit. But **I'd like to** be able to speak it well.*
Janya:	ah . . . mah láir-o mah láir-o kOOn Sŏm-chai glùp mah láir-o
	Here he is! Khun Somchai is back.
Somchai:	ah . . . sa-wùt dee há kOOn Frank **bpen yung-ngai bâhng?**
	*Ah, hello, Frank. **How are things?***

Introductions and greetings

sa-wùt dee krúp/kâ	Hello, good morning/afternoon/ evening/goodbye
sa-bai dee lĕr krúp/ká?	How are you?
bpen yung-ngai bâhng?	How are things?
sa-bai dee	I'm fine
kOOn chêu a-rai krúp/ká?	What's your name?
pŏm (chún) chêu . . .	My name is . . .
nêe fairn pŏm	This is my wife
nêe săh-mee	This is my husband
nêe pêu-un	This is my friend
yin dee têe dâi róo-jùk	Pleased to meet you
chern kâhng nai ná krúp/ká	Please come in

sa-wùt dee krúp/kâ is a formal greeting which can be used at any time of the day; unlike English, Thai does not use a different greeting form for different periods of the day. **sa-wùt dee** can also mean 'goodbye'. **sa-bai dee lĕr krúp/ká?** (Are you well?) is a rather formal expression, more appropriate for using with relative strangers, than **bpen yung-ngai bâhng?** Both questions can be answered by **sa-bai dee** (I'm fine). Notice that Somchai uses the informal polite particle **há** instead of **krúp** when he greets Frank.

yòo meu-ung tai bpen yung-ngai?/what do you think of Thailand?

Conversations in Thai will at first tend to follow a fairly predictable pattern which will include compliments about your command of Thai and questions about where you come from and what you think of Thailand. The latter requires a short complimentary response and not a list of personal gripes nor your reflections on the state of the Thai economy! See how well Frank handles a typical conversation in a taxi. He limits his responses to short manageable phrases, and even manages to seize the initiative and ask the taxi-driver about himself.

Taxi:	**tum-mai** kOOn pôot tai gèng?
	***Why** do you speak Thai (so) well?*
Frank:	mâi gèng ròrk
	I don't.
Taxi:	gèng si krúp **bpen kon a-may-ri-gun** châi mái krúp?
	*Yes you do. **You're American** aren't you?*
Frank:	mâi châi **bpen kon ung-grìt** krúp
	*No. **I'm English.***
Taxi:	or . . . bpen kon ung-grìt lěr? **yòo meu-ung tai bpen yung-ngai?**
	*Oh, you're English, eh? **How are you finding Thailand?***
Frank:	chôrp mâhk krúp **sa-nÒOk dee dtàir** rót dtìt mâhk ná **kOOn mah jàhk năi?**
	*I like it. **It's great. But** the traffic is very bad. **Where do you come from?***
Taxi:	bpen kon ee-săhn mah jàhk jung-wùt nŏrng-kai róo-jùk mái?
	I'm a North-Easterner. I come from Nongkhai Province. Do you know it?
Frank:	róo-jùk yòo glâi glâi bpra-tâyt lao châi mái?
	Yes. It's near Laos, isn't it?

Making conversation

meu-ung tai	Thailand
pŏm (chún) mah têe-o meu-ung tai	I'm on holiday in Thailand
pŏm (chún) mah tÓO-rá têe meu-ung tai	I'm on business in Thailand
pah-săh tai	Thai (language)
pôot pah-săh tai dâi nít-nòy	I can speak a little Thai
nít-nòy	a little
tâo-nún	only
kOOn pôot pah-săh ung-grìt bpen mái?	Can you speak English?
kOOn yòo meu-ung tai nahn tâo-rài?	How long have you been in Thailand?
yòo meu-ung tai bpen yung-ngai?	How are you finding Thailand?
chôrp mâhk	I like it
sa-nÒOk dee	It's great (literally 'It's good fun')

sa-nÒOk means 'fun' or 'to have fun'. The idea that everything should be **sa-nÒOk** is regarded by many commentators on Thailand as part of the essence of 'Thai-ness' and an important concept in understanding Thai attitudes and their outlook on life.

Where are you from? (kOOn mah jàhk năi?)

bpen kon ung-grìt	I'm English/British
. . . a-may-ri-gun	. . . American
. . . tai	. . . Thai
. . . fa-rùng-sàyt	. . . French
. . . yer-ra-mun	. . . German
. . . yêe-bpÒOn	. . . Japanese

the way it works

You

There are lots of words for 'you' in Thai. Thais will take into account the age and status of the person they are talking to and their own relationship to that person. The safest word for the foreigner to use is **kOOn**. Notice that Somchai and Janya address Jill and Frank as **kOOn** Jill and **kOOn** Frank instead of just **kOOn** when they are speaking directly to them. Using the personal name with **kOOn** sounds more friendly and less formal.

Can (. . . bpen mái?)

In the previous section, you met the verb **bpen** which, when followed by a noun, means 'to be'. When it occurs at the end of a sentence, however, it means 'can', 'to be able to', 'to know how to do something'. When talking about knowledge of foreign languages, Thais use both **bpen** and **dâi**.

kOOn pôot pah-săh tai **dâi** mái?	Can/Do you speak Thai?
dâi/mâi dâi	Yes/No
kOOn pôot pah-săh tai **bpen** mái?	Can/Do you speak Thai?
bpen/mâi bpen	Yes/No

láir-o

You may already have noticed the word **láir-o** in the expression **gôr láir-o gun** (I'll settle for . . .), and to mean 'and' (**fairn-dtâh láir-o gôr bee-a** fanta and beer). When it occurs at the end of a sentence, **láir-o** indicates that the action of the verb has been completed. It can often be translated in English as 'already' or by a past tense of the verb:

káo glùp mah **láir-o**	He has returned/He's back.
chún yòo meu-ung tai nahn **láir-o**	I've lived in Thailand a long time.

More expressions of time

In expressing the length or duration of time in Thai, there is no word to correspond to the English 'for'.

chún yòo meu-ung tai **sŏrng ah-tít**	I've been in Thailand *for two weeks.*
káo ree-un pah-săh tai **lăi bpee**	He's studied Thai *for many years.*
pŏm bpai **wun dee-o** tâo-nún	I only went *for one (a single) day.*

Not at all (mâi . . . ler-ee)

The word **ler-ee** is used to add emphasis to negative expressions:

mâi pairng **ler-ee**	(It's) *not at all* expensive.
mâi a-ròy **ler-ee**	(It's) *not at all* delicious.
mâi chôrp **ler-ee**	(I) *don't like it at all.*
mâi sa-nÒOk **ler-ee**	(It) *wasn't* fun *at all.*

Reduplication

You will often hear words spoken twice in Thai; sometimes Thais will carry the convention into English, and you might, for example, hear a shopkeeper assuring you that two different items are 'same same'! Generally, the reduplication does not significantly change the meaning; it simply sounds more natural. Here are some examples:

kŏr bee-a **yen yen** nòy?	Could I have a *cold* beer?
yòo **glâi glâi** rohng rairm	It's *near* the hotel
pairng **jing jing**	It's *really* expensive (**jing** literally 'true')

However, the first word of the reduplicated pair may be pronounced with an exaggerated high tone, irrespective of its normal tone, for emphatic effect. This tends to be more common in the speech of women:

páirng pairng	*Ever so* expensive!
a-róy a-ròy	*Ever so* tasty!
chórp chôrp	I *really* like it

things to do

1 Practise greeting the following people:
   1 Somchai: Say hello.
   2 Janya: Say hello and ask how she is.
   3 Chartchai: Say hello and ask how things are.
   4 Malee: Introduce yourself and say you are pleased to meet her.

2 Here are some of the questions that you are sure to be asked when you are in Thailand. How would you respond?
   1 kOOn pôot pah-săh tai bpen mái?
   2 kOOn yòo meu-ung tai nahn mái?
   3 meu-ung tai bpen yung-ngai?

3 kOOn bpen kon a-rai? How would these people express their nationality?

4 Some Thais are being very complimentary about your command of Thai. Modestly tell them you're not nearly as good as they seem to think (If you listen to this section on the tape you will hear the third and fourth speakers use the 'forced' high tone.) The first example has been done for you: you don't have to repeat the reduplication in your answer.
   1 kOOn pôot tai gèng krúp   3 kOOn pôot tai géng gèng
     You: *mâi* gèng *ròrk* krúp   You: . . .
   2 kOOn pôot tai chút krúp   4 kOOn pôot tai chút chút
     You: . . .   You: . . .

TALKING ABOUT YOURSELF
AND YOUR FAMILY

Thai small-talk is generally more personal than its English equivalent. This expression of interest in the other person is an excellent ice-breaker and smoothes the initial stage of friendship; at the same time it serves the valuable function of establishing relative status which is important for Thais to know in order to be able to behave appropriately in future.

Be prepared to accept that you will be asked personal questions that would be quite inappropriate back home. Don't be surprised by questions about your salary and if you are married and do not have children, you may be asked why not – and more – which, it should be pointed out, is not necessarily entirely appropriate in Thailand. Sometimes people's curiosity gets the better of them! Usually a smile and feigned misunderstanding will be sufficient to change the subject and, in any case, there is no real obligation to give truthful answers in such situations.

kŏr-tôht/I hope you don't mind me asking but . . .

After lunch, Somchai is catching up on news from Frank:

Somchai: dtorn née kOOn Frank **tum ngahn a-rai?**
What do you do now Frank?

Frank: **bpen núk tÓO-rá-gìt   tum ngahn yòo gùp bor-ri-sùt lék lék**
têe lorn-dorn
I'm a businessman. I'm working for a small company in London.

Somchai:	láir-o fairn lâ tum ngahn **rěu bplào?**
	*How about your wife? Does she work (**or not**)?*
Frank:	tum krúp bpen kroo **sǒrn yòo têe** rohng ree-un yài yài têe lorn-dorn
	*Yes. She's a teacher. **She's teaching in** a large school in London.*
Somchai:	kǒr-tôht mee lôok **láir-o rěu yung?**
	*I hope you don't mind me asking, but do you have any children **yet**?*
Frank:	yung krúp
	Not yet.

What do you do (tum ngahn a-rai?)

bpen núk tÓÓ-rá-gìt	I'm a businessman/woman
pa-núk-ngahn bor-ri-sùt	I'm a company employee
mǒr	I'm a doctor
kroo	I'm a teacher
núk sèuk-sǎh	I'm a student

pǒm (chún) tum ngahn nai . . .	I work in . . .
ta-nah-kahn	. . . a bank
orp-fít	. . . an office
ráhn	. . . a shop
têe bâhn	. . . at home

While Frank chats to Somchai about work, Jill, despite her limited Thai, is asking all the right kind of questions to keep the conversation flowing as Janya shows her some snapshots from the family album:

Jill:	nêe **krai** ká?
	***Who's** this?*
Janya:	nêe dee-chún gùp **pêe-sǎo** chêu Jin-dah pêe-sǎo dtàirng ngahn láir-o mee **lôok sǎhm kon**
	*This is me with my **elder sister**. Her name's Jinda. My elder sister is married. She's got **three children**.*
Jill:	pôo-yǐng **rěu** pôo-chai ká?
	*Boys **or** girls?*
Janya:	pôo-chai kon nèung pôo-yǐng sǒrng kon
	One boy. Two girls.
Jill:	ah-yÓÓ tâo-rài ká?
	How old are they?
Janya:	pôo-chai ah-yÓÓ sǒrng kòo-up tâo-nún **nâh rúk** jing jing pôo-yǐng ah-yÓÓ jèt kòo-up gùp bpàirt kòo-up
	*The boy is only two. He's really **cute**. The girls are seven and eight.*

kŏr-tôht kOOn Jill mee **pêe-nórng** gèe kon?
*I hope you don't mind me asking, but how many **brothers and sisters** do you have?*

Jill: mee **nórng-chai** kon nèung **nórng-săo** kon nèung láir **pêe-chai** kon nèung
*I have one **younger brother**, one **younger sister** and one **older brother**.*

Boys and girls, brothers and sisters, sons and daughters

Each of these terms consists of two words in Thai, the second of which indicates gender. Often you will hear Thais referring to a brother or sister simply as **pêe** or **nórng** and it can take some time to work out whether it is a brother or sister that is being referred to.

pôo-chai	boy (literally 'one who is-male')
pôo-yĭng	girl ('one who is-female')
lôok-chai	son ('child-male')
lôok-săo	daughter ('child-female')
pêe-nórng	brothers and sisters ('ones who are older-ones who are younger')
pêe-chai	older brother ('one who is older-male')
pêe-săo	older sister ('one who is older-female')
nórng-chai	younger brother ('one who is younger-male')
nórng-săo	younger sister ('one who is younger-female')

USEFUL WORDS AND PHRASES

nêe krai?	Who's this?
mee	to have; there is/there are
gùp	with
sòht	unmarried/single
dtàirng ngahn láir-o	married
kOOn dtàirng ngahn láir-o rĕu yung?	Are you married?
kOOn mee lôok láir-o rĕu yung?	Do you have any children?
yung/yung mâi mee	No/Not yet
ah-yÓO tâo-rài?	How old are you?
ah-yÓO	age
mâir	mother
pôr	father
pôr mâir	parents

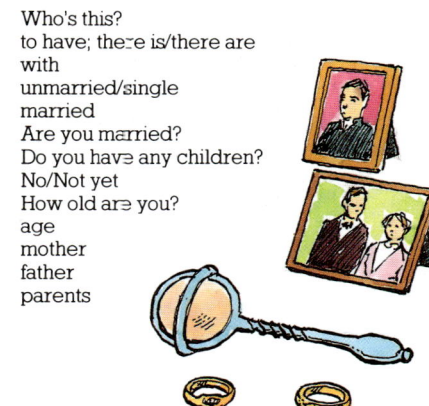

the way it works

An important classifier

The classifier for people is **kon** which also means 'person'. (You have met it already in the phrase **bpen kon ung-grit** – literally 'I am an English person'.)

lôok sǎhm **kon**	three children
kroo **kon** nèung	one/a teacher
núk tÓO-rá-gìt hâh **kon**	five businessmen

Note that the word **lôok** means children in the sense of 'offspring'. In phrases like 'children nowadays', 'that child over there', etc. Thai uses the word **dèk**. You might ask a teacher how many **dèk** she had in her class, but if you wanted to know how many children of her own she had, you would use **lôok**.

He, she, and they

In the translations of the dialogues you will notice that the words 'he', 'she' and 'they' appear with no corresponding word in the Thai. The word **káo** can be used for all three words, but as with Thai pronouns generally, it is frequently omitted.

How old are you? (ah-yÓO tâo-rài?)

To state a person's age use the pattern:

person + *ah-yÓO* + *number* + **kòo-up/bpee** (*years*)

Notice that there are two words for 'years': **kòo-up** is used when talking about children up to the age of about thirteen or fourteen but after that **bpee** is used.

pêe-chai ah-yÓO yêe-sìp-sŏrng **bpee**	(Her) older brother is 22
lôok-sǎo ah-yÓO bpàirt **kòo-up**	(My) daughter is eight

More question forms

. . . rĕu bplào   This could be literally translated as '. . . or not?' It is an extremely common question form in Thai and not nearly as brusque as the literal English translation suggests. To answer 'yes', repeat the verb in the question and to answer 'no', just say **bplào**.

37

bpai **rěu bplào**?   Are you going (or not)?
bpai/bplào   Yes/No

. . . (láir-o) rěu yung?   This expression literally means '. . . already' or 'not yet' and is used at the end of a question when asking whether someone has done something. To answer 'yes', repeat the verb and then the word **láir-o**; to answer 'no', simply say **yung**.

dtàirng ngahn **láir-o rěu yung**?   Are you married **yet**?
dtàirng (ngahn) láir-o/yung   Yes/No
(**láir-o** may be omitted in the question form: dtàirng ngahn **rěu yung?**)

things to do

3.5   Janya is telling Jill about her parents. Can you understand what she says? (Use the vocabulary at the back of the book to find any unfamiliar words.)
    What nationality is her father?
    What's his job?
    Where does her mother come from?
    What's her job?

nêe kOOn pôr kOOn mâir kâ   kOOn pôr mah jàhk bpra-tâyt jeen dtàir yòo meu-ung tai nahn láir-o   bpen pôo-jùt-gahn bor-ri-sùt têe jung-wùt sŏng-klǎh nai pâhk dtâi   kOOn mâir bpen kon tai   mah jàhk pâhk dtâi jung-wùt poo-gèt   kOOn mâir mâi tum ngahn   bpen mâir bâhn

(A full translation is given in the Key on p. 82.)

Notice that when Janya refers to her parents, she uses the polite title **kOOn** in front of the word for 'father' (**pôr**) and 'mother' (**mâir**).

3.6   Next, Janya shows you this picture.

How would you ask:
1   who it is?
2   what his name is?
3   how old he is?
4   what job he does?

3.7   You are visiting a friend and a Thai strikes up a conversation. See if you can answer his questions.
1   Sŏm-sùk: tum ngahn a-rai?
                [Say you work in an office in London]
2   Sŏm-sùk: dtàirng ngahn láir-o rěu yung?
                [Say yes you are married]
3   Sŏm-sùk: kŏr-tôht   mee lôok láir-o rěu yung?
                [Say yes you have a boy and a girl]
4   Sŏm-sùk: ah-yÓO tâo-rài krúp?
                [Explain that the boy is ten and the girl is only three]

SIGHTSEEING AND ENTERTAINMENT

Tourism   Thailand's popularity as a tourist destination continues to grow and tourism has for a number of years ranked as one of the country's major industries. A first visit to the country is typically spent mainly in Bangkok, with perhaps short trips to seaside resorts such as Pattaya, Hua Hin or Cha-am, and possibly a longer excursion to Thailand's second largest city, Chiangmai, in the north, or to Phuket in the south. Many visitors quickly become infatuated with the country and the charm and friendliness of its people, and on subsequent visits explore further afield.

There is no shortage of books in English offering advice on where to go, how to get there and what to see and do once you arrive in Thailand. In Bangkok, (**grOOng-tâyp** in Thai, which means literally 'the city of angels') visitors tend to start by seeking out the images popularly associated with the country; orange-robed monks carrying alms bowls through deserted streets at daybreak, the dazzlingly bright tiled temple roofs with their fearsome-looking demon guards, the refined gestures of classical dancers, now most readily seen in restaurants, and the less wholesome nightlife. Invaluable aids for the visitor who wishes to venture a little beyond the normal tourist sights are the excellent sketch maps of Bangkok and Chiangmai (readily available in Bangkok bookshops and larger hotels) which provide a wealth of detail and additional information of the kind not normally found in guidebooks, including places that are suitable for children.

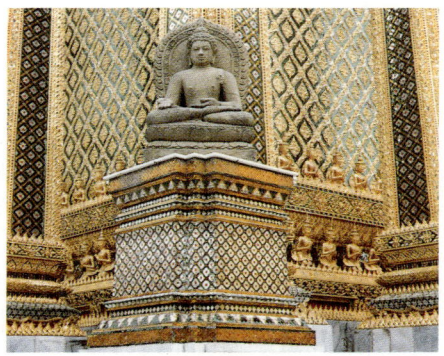

Don't be surprised if you find some places charging foreigners a considerably higher admission fee than Thais, or levying an entrance fee on foreigners where Thais are admitted free. If such officially sanctioned double-standards offend your sense of fairness, remind yourself of what the minimum daily wage is in Thailand.

wun née yàhk bpai têe-o têe-nǎi?/where do you want to go today?

Janya has offered to act as a guide for Jill and Frank and is asking them what they'd like to do:

Janya: wun née yàhk bpai têe-o têe-nǎi ká?
Where would you like to go today?

Jill: **yàhk bpai têe-o** wút kâ
***I'd like to go and visit** some temples.*

Janya: kOOn Jill bpai têe-o wút prá-gâir-o rěu yung?
Have you been to the Temple of the Emerald Buddha yet?

Jill: yung kâ
No.

Janya: gôr . . . **bpai têe-o** wút prá-gâir-o gòrn **dee mái**?
*Well . . . **shall we visit** the Temple of the Emerald Buddha first?*

Frank: láir-o **bpai** pi-pít-ta-pun hàirng châht **dâi mái**?
*And then **can we go** to the National Museum?*

Janya: dâi kâ   pi-pít-ta-pun yòo glâi glâi wút prá-gâir-o
Yes. The museum is close to the Temple of the Emerald Buddha.

What would you like to do?

pǒm (chún) yàhk ja . . .	I'd like to . . .
. . . **dee mái**?	Shall we . . . ? (literally 'would it be good to . . . ?)
. . . **dâi mái**?	Can we . . . ?

bpai têe-o wút/visiting a temple

At some stage you are sure to go to or be taken to a Thai temple. Dress appropriately and watch carefully for parts of the temple where you are expected to remove your shoes. Since some temples do not permit photographs to be taken, it is considerate to check with an official first.

Janya is taking Frank and Jill round a temple:

Frank: têe-nêe **hâhm** tài rôop rěu bplào krúp?
*Is it **forbidden** to take photos here?*

Janya: **chún mâi sâhp kâ** dtôrng tǎhm jâo nâh-têe gòrn dee gwàh . . . er kǒr-tôht kâ têe-nêe tài rôop dâi mái ká?
I don't know. It's best to ask the official first. Er . . . excuse me. Can you take photos here?

Official: dâi krúp dtàir chôo-ay bòrk fa-rùng wâh dtôrng tòrt rorng táo kâhng nai
Yes. But please tell the farangs ['westerners'] that they have to take their shoes off inside.

Janya: kâ tài rôop dâi kâ kOOn Frank káo mâi hâhm **sǒo-ay mái** ká?
*Right. You can take a picture, Frank. It's not prohibited. **Do you like it?** [literally: Is it beautiful?]*

Jill: sǒo-ay mâhk kâ
It's very beautiful.

Janya: sǒo-ay ná ngêe-up dee
Yes, it is beautiful. It's nice and quiet in here.

Sightseeing

yàhk ja bpai têe-o . . .	I'd like to visit . . .
. . . wút X	. . . Temple X
. . . dta-làht náhm	. . . the Floating Market
. . . meu-ung boh-rahn	. . . the Ancient City
. . . sǒo-un sǎhm prahn	. . . the Rose Garden
. . . reu-a	. . . take a boat trip
. . . pút-ta-yah	. . . Pattaya
. . . chai ta-lay	. . . the seaside
kǒr dtǒo-a sǎhm bai	Could I have three tickets please?
kǒr tài rôop nòy dâi mái?	Can I take a photo?
yàhk ja bpai doo nǔng	I'd like to see a film
. . . rum tai	. . . Thai dancing (classical)
. . . moo-ay tai	. . . Thai boxing
. . . la-korn tai	. . . Thai drama (classical)
rôrp sǎhm tÔOm	the 9 p.m. *show*
yàhk ja bpai fung don-dtree	I'd like to go and listen to some music
rohng nǔng/ rohng pâhp-pa-yon	cinema
rohng la-korn (hàirng châht)	theatre (national)
pí-pít-ta-pun (hàirng châht)	museum (national)
hǒr sa-mÒOt (hàirng châht)	library (national)
sa-nǎhm gee-lah (hàirng châht)	stadium (national)
bor-ri-sùt num têe-o	tour company
ngêe-up	quiet, peaceful
gào	old
sǒo-ay	beautiful
yài	large
lék	small
mái	wooden

SPORT

Most westerners find Thailand extremely hot and indulging in vigorous athletic activity is not usually a high priority. However, swimming in hotel pools (there are few public pools in Thailand) is an effective way of keeping cool while tennis and more recently jogging have become increasingly popular during the cooler parts of the day, just after daybreak and immediately before dusk. Equipment for water sports is available for hire at popular seaside resorts.

Thais themselves play all the popular international sports such as football, basketball, badminton and so on, as well as a number of traditional games and athletic activities. Of these, the best known is Thai boxing or **moo-ay tai**, in which contestants are allowed to use their feet, knees and elbows as well as their fists. In Bangkok, Thai boxing contests attract huge crowds at the two major boxing stadiums, Ratchadamnoen Stadium and Lumpini Stadium.

kOOn chôrp lên gee-lah a-rai bâhng?/which sports do you enjoy?

Frank, Jill and Janya have stopped for a rest and are chatting over a cool drink:

Janya:	kOOn Frank chôrp lên gee-lah a-rai bâhng ká?
	Which sports do you enjoy Frank?
Frank:	gôr . . . chôrp ten-nít láir górf krúp
	Well . . . I like tennis and golf.
Janya:	mee sa-nǎhm górf yòo tǎir-o tǎir-o bâhn rao bpai lên gùp kOOn Sǒmchai gôr dâi kOOn Jill chôrp lên gee-lah mái?
	There's a golf course near our house. You could go and play with Khun Somchai. Do you like sports, Jill?
Jill:	chôrp kâ chôrp ten-nít měu-un gun dtàir lên mâi kôy gèng chôrp wâi náhm mâhk gwàn
	Yes, I like tennis too but I'm not very good. I prefer swimming.
Janya:	pêu-un mee sà wâi náhm têe bâhn wun lǔng bpai wâi náhm dôo-ay gun dee mái?
	A friend of mine has a pool at her house. Another day shall we go swimming together?
Jill:	dee kâ kong ja sa-nÒOk
	Yes. That would be fun.

Sporting activities

gee-lah	sport
lên	play
chôrp lên	I like playing . . .
lên . . . mâi kôy gèng	I'm not very good at . .
fÓOt-born	football
báht	basketball
bàird-min-dtûn	badminton

jórk-gîng	jogging
moo-ay	boxing
sa-năhm moo-ay	boxing stadium
sa-năhm máh	race-course
górf	golf
sa-năhm górf	golf course
ten-nít	tennis
sa-năhm ten-nít	tennis court
wâi náhm	swimming
sà wâi náhm	swimming pool

the way it works

Prohibition

hâhm means 'forbid' and appears in prohibition notices, such as 'No Smoking', 'No Rubbish', 'No Parking', etc. This is what the word looks like in Thai script . . .

ห้าม

. . . and here are some examples of common prohibition notices for recognition purposes . . .

ห้ามเข้า
No Entry

ห้ามทิ้งขยะ
No Rubbish

ห้ามสูบบุหรี่
No Smoking

ห้ามจอด
No Parking

fa-rung

The word **fa-rung** refers to people of European descent; although it describes people of a particular colour it is a neutral word and carries no racialist undertones.

things to do

4.1 If you have the cassette, listen to Jill discussing her plans for tomorrow with Janya.
1 What does she want to do?
2 What obstacle is there to her plans?
3 What advice and assistance does Janya offer?
(The script of the conversation between Jill and Janya appears in the Key on p. 82 together with a translation.)

2 True or false?
1 Jill chôrp lên górf
2 Sŏm-chai wâi náhm mâi kôy gèng
3 Frank chôrp lên ten-nít
4 Jun-yah chôrp bpai lên jórk-gîng

CHANGING MONEY

Currency exchange   Banks in Thailand are open from 8.30 a.m. to 3.30 p.m. on weekdays but are closed at weekends. In Bangkok, however, many of the major banks have currency exchange kiosks outside the main building and some of these are open seven days a week until 8 p.m.

45

Money can also be changed on arrival in Thailand at Don Muang airport where there is a 24-hour service. Major hotels also operate currency exchange facilities but these are usually at a less favourable rate. Credit cards are becoming more widely accepted although most shops will still insist on payment in cash.

Thai currency   The basic unit of Thai currency is the **baht**. The baht is subdivided into 100 **satang**; 25 satang (the smallest coin) is also known as 1 **saleung**.

Thai banknotes come in denominations of 500 baht (purple) 100 baht (red) 50 baht (blue) 20 baht (green) and 10 baht (brown). The coins are 5 baht and 1 baht which are silver, and 50 satang and 25 satang which are bronze.

têe ta-na-kahn/at the bank

Jill:	**yàhk ja lâirk-bplèe-un chék dern tahng dâi mái?** *I'd like to change some traveller's cheques, please.*
Clerk:	kǒr doo núng-sěu dern tahng láir chék dern tahng krúp *Could I see your passport and traveller's cheques?*
Jill:	ùt-dtrah lâirk bplèe-un tâo-rài wun née? *What's today's exchange rate?*
Clerk:	sèe-sìp-sèe bàht dtòr nèung bporn **chôo-ay sen chêu têe-nêe** *Forty four baht to the pound. **Please sign here**.*

Money

ngern	money
ta-nah-kahn	bank
ta-nah-bùt	banknote
chék dern tahng	traveller's cheque
bùt kray-dìt	credit card
rěe-un	coin
bporn	pound
dorn-lâh	dollar
núng-sěu dern tahng	passport

GOING OUT FOR A MEAL

Thais delight in eating out and there seem to be restaurants everywhere, catering for a wide range of income levels. A basic decision when going out to eat is whether you are going to order your food individually or whether you are going to order rice and side-dishes which you will share. If people are in a hurry, on their own or anxious to eat cheaply, they will probably opt for the former but a special invitation to a meal would normally involve the latter. Larger restaurants (**ráhn ah-hăhn**) will provide menus in both Thai and English; small noodle shops (**ráhn gŏo-ay dtĕe-o**) are more likely to have the menu on a large blackboard on the wall, but in Thai only.

If you go out to eat with Thai friends, you may find yourself invited to choose one of the dishes. Don't make the mistake of believing that your selection is for your exclusive consumption; your choice is expected to take into consideration the dishes already selected, so as to create a suitable variety of dishes. If you are not quite sure what an appropriate order would be, you can evade responsibility by saying **hâi kOOn X sùng dee gwàh** (I'd better let Khun X order). But watch the combinations that Thais select so that in the future you don't order the Thai equivalent of a potato sandwich or fish fingers with Yorkshire pudding!

เนื้อ	Beef dishes
เนื้อผัดน้ำมันหอย NEAU PaD NAM MUN HOI	Fried beef with oyster sauce
เนื้อผัดพริก NEAU PAD PRIG	Fried beef with fresh chillies
เนื้อย่างน้ำตก NEAU YANG NUM TOK	Char-grilled beef with fresh chillies
เนื้อทอดกระเทียมพริกไทย NEAU TOD KRATIEM PRIG THAI	Beef fried with pepper and garlic
เนื้อสะ เต๊ะแบบกวางตุ้ง NEAU STEAK CANTONESE STYLE	Beef steak with onions in tomato sauce
เนื้อผัด เต้าเจี้ยว NEAU PAD TAO JIEW	Fried beef in black bean sauce
เนื้อผัดขิง NEAU PAD KING	Fried beef with fresh ginger
เนื้อ เปรี้ยวหวาน NEAU PRIEW WAN	Sweet and sour beef
เนื้อผัดหน่อไม้ NEAU PAD NOR MAI	Fried beef with bamboo shoots

Thais use a spoon and fork for eating, not chopsticks (although chopsticks are used in the thousands of Chinese noodle shops). Rice is served onto each person's plate – if you have to serve yourself, don't take too much first time: you will find your friends take second and third helpings and order another large bowl if necessary – and then a spoonful or two is taken from one or two of the side-dishes, mixed with rice and eaten. A meal is a constant 'dipping-in' process rather than a single massive foray. (An exception to this is the lunch time buffets held in some Bangkok hotels where a wide variety and large quantity of Thai and western foods can be sampled relatively cheaply.) Some restaurants will provide a serving spoon for each of the side-dishes, or they may provide an individual serving spoon and bowl for the curry, but if they do not, you simply use the spoon you are eating with. Many standard Thai dishes are extremely hot to the western palate so it is useful to know how to ask that the chef go easy on the chillies (**mâi ao pèt mâhk ná**). Wine is only available in western-style restaurants and does not go well with Thai food.

The bill is brought at the end of the meal and is collected by the host. 'Going Dutch' – or 'American Share' as it is called in Thailand – is considered rather tasteless. Don't offer to pay your part of the bill, which would be an insult to the host (and to the other guests, if you weren't planning to treat them too); and don't worry because there will doubtless be a chance for you to reciprocate at a later date! A small tip is customary.

têe ráhn ah-hăhn/at the restaurant

On Thursday evening, Somchai and Janya take Jill and Frank out to a restaurant.

Waiter:	sùng rĕu yung krúp?
	Have you ordered yet?
Somchai:	yung **kŏr doo may-noo nòy**
	*Not yet. **Can I see the menu?***
Waiter:	nêe krúp
	Here you are.
Somchai:	er . . . ja sùng yung-ngai dee? kOOn Jill chôrp tahn a-rai?
	Mm . . . What shall we order? What do you like, Jill?
Jill:	**a-rai gôr dâi** kâ **hâi kOOn Sŏm-chai sùng dee gwàh**
	Anything. It's better that you order, Khun Somchai.
Somchai:	kOOn Frank tahn pèt bpen mái?
	Can you eat hot food?
Frank:	bpen krúp
	Yes.

Somchai:	. . . gôr . . . kŏr dtôm yum gÔOng **mâi ao pèt mâhk**
(to waiter)	**ná** láir-o gôr . . . mŏo pùt kǐng lair-o bplah bprêe-o wǎhn láir-o gôr gairng gài ao kâo dôo-ay ná
	*Right . . . I'd like a shrimp 'tom yam'. **Not too hot, O.K.?** And . . . pork fried with ginger, and sweet and sour fish, and chicken curry. We'd like rice, too.*
Waiter:	**rúp náhm a-rai krúp?**
	What would you like to drink?
Jill:	kŏr bpép-sêe kâ?
	Can I have Pepsi, please?
Somchai:	gôr . . . ao bpép-sêe sŏrng gâir-ɔ láir-o bee-a sŏrng kòo-ut
	O.K. Two glasses of Pepsi and two beers.
Janya:	chún mâi ao bpép-sêe **ao núm sôm dee gwàh**
	*I don't want Pepsi. **I'd rather have orange juice.***

After the main course, the waiter returns:

Waiter:	**rúp** kŏrng wâhn **mái krúp?**
	***Would you like** any dessert?*
Janya:	mee a-rai bâhng ká?
	What do you have?
Waiter:	gôr mee ka-nŏm mee pŏn-la-mái láir-o gôr mee ai dtǐm
	Well, there's sweet, there's fruit and ice-cream.
Janya:	kOOn Jill ker-ee tahn ka-nŏm tai mái?
	Have you ever eaten Thai dessert?
Jill:	ker-ee krúng dee-o kâ **mâi kôy** chôrp **tâo-rài** mâi kôy a-ròy
	*Yes. Once. **I don't** like them **very much**. They don't taste very nice.*
Janya:	lĕr? gôr . . . mee pŏn-la-mái a-rai bâhng ká?
	Really? Well . . . what fruit is there?
Waiter:	mee ma-la-gor sùp-bpa-rót láir-o gôr dtairng moh
	There's papaya, pineapple and water melon.

Most Thai men smoke and in Thailand smoking is generally regarded as manly (in men) and sophisticated (in *some* women).

After the meal, Somchai takes out his cigarettes:

Somchai:	**sòop bOO-rèe mái** krúp?
	Do you smoke?
Frank:	pŏm mâi sòop krúp lêrk láir-o
	I don't smoke. I've given it up.
Somchai:	láir-o kOOn Jill lâ krúp
	And how about you, Jill?
Jill:	sòop mâi bpen kâ
	I don't smoke.

Somchai: kOOn krúp!   kǒr têe kèe-a bOO-rèe nòy   kǒr mái kèet
dôo-ay ná
*Waiter! Can I have an ash-tray, please? Can I have some
matches, too?*

Do you mind if I smoke?

bOO-rèe	cigarette
mái kèet	match
têe kèe-a bOO-rèe	ash-tray
fai cháirk	lighter
kǒr sòop bOO-rèe nòy dâi mái?	Do you mind if I smoke?
sòop bOO-rèe mái krúp/ká?	Would you like a cigarette?/Do you smoke?
pǒm (chún) mâi sòop krúp/kâ	I don't smoke, thank you
pǒm (chún) sòop mâi bpen krúp/kâ	I don't smoke (literally: 'I can't smoke')
pǒm (chún) lêrk láir-o	I've given it up

SOME COMMON THAI DISHES

Curries and soups

gairng	'wet' curry (i.e. a lot of liquid)
pa-nairng	'dry' curry (i.e. served with little or no liquid)
gairng gài	chicken curry
gairng pèt	hot, spicy curry
gairng mút-sa-mùn	'Muslim' curry (southern Thai chicken curry)
gairng jèut	a bland, clear soup
dtôm yum gÔOng/bplah	shrimp/fish *tom yam* (spicy shrimp/fish soup)

Meat and fish

gài	chicken
néu-a	beef
mǒo	pork
bpèt	duck
bpoo	crab
bplah	fish
gÔOng	shrimp
gÔOng gâhm grahm	lobster
bplah-mèuk	squid
gài/néu-a/mǒo pùt kǐng	chicken/beef/pork fried with ginger
. . . pùt prík	. . . fried with chillies
bpèt/gài yâhng	roast (barbecued) duck/chicken
mǒo/bplah pùt bprêe-o wǎhn	sweet and sour chicken/fish
. . . pùt nòr-mái	. . . fried with bamboo shoots
. . . pùt bai ga-prao	. . . fried with basil leaves
. . . pùt núm mun hǒy	. . . fried in oyster sauce
. . . pa-lóh	. . . stewed in soy sauce
. . . tôrt gra-tee-um prík tai	. . . fried with garlic and pepper

Egg dishes

kài	egg
kài dao	fried egg
kài jee-o	deep-fried omelette
kài yút-sâi	stuffed omelette
kài lôok kĕr-ee	'son-in-law eggs' (hard-boiled eggs garnished with various condiments)
kài lôo-uk	very soft-boiled/semi-raw egg drunk out of a glass

Rice and rice dishes

kâo	rice
kâo sŏo-ay	boiled rice
kâo bplào	plain rice
kâo pùt	fried rice
kâo nĕe-o	sticky rice
kâo pùt gài/gÔOng/mŏo/bpoo	chicken/shrimp/pork/crab fried rice
kâo nâh bpèt/gài	duck/chicken rice
kâo mŏo dairng	red pork rice
kâo dtôm	rice gruel, rice 'porridge'

Noodles and noodle dishes

gŏo-ay dtĕe-o	noodles made from rice flour
gŏo-ay dtĕe-o náhm	noodle soup
gŏo-ay dtĕe-o hâirng	boiled 'dry' noodles (i.e. without soup)
ba-mèe	egg noodles
ba-mèe náhm	egg noodle soup
ba-mèe hâirng	boiled 'dry' egg noodles
wÓOn sên	transparent noodles
mèe gròrp	crispy noodles
pùt see éw	Chinese-style fried noodles in soy sauce
pùt tai	Thai-style fried noodles

Miscellaneous

mŏo sa-dtáy	pork *satay* (thin strips of charcoal-grilled pork)
tôrt mun	*tort mun* (finely minced shrimp or fish fried in batter with spices)
bpor bpée-a	Thai spring roll
yum	a kind of Thai 'salad'
yum néu-a	beef 'salad'
yum wÓOn sên	transparent noodle 'salad'
sôm dtum	a kind of Thai 'salad' made with green papaya
kŏrng wâhn	dessert
ka-nŏm	cake, sweet, dessert
ai dtĭm	ice-cream

USEFUL WORDS AND PHRASES

rúp a-rai?	What would you like to eat?
rúp náhm a-rai?	What would you like to drink?
kŏr doo may-noo nòy?	Can I see the menu?
sùng	to order
chôrp tahn a-rai?	What do you like?
chôrp ah-hăhn tai (mâhk)	I like Thai food (very much)
mâi kôy chôrp tâo-rài	I don't like it very much
pèt mâhk mái?	Is it very spicy?
pŏm (chún) mâi gin néu-a	I don't eat meat

the way it works

Polite language: choosing the right word

When Jill and Frank went into the noodle shop to get a drink on Tuesday morning the girl serving asked them **ao a-rai ká?** (What would you like?) In the rather more expensive restaurant that Somchai has taken them to, the waiter is more deferential, using the verb **rúp** instead of **ao**. However, it is perfectly appropriate for Somchai to use **ao** when he is ordering food. When Somchai asks Jill and Frank what they would like to eat, he uses the polite word **tahn** for 'to eat' while Jill uses the less formal word **gin**.

Expressing a preference

dee gwàh literally means 'better' and is used with the verb **ao** or **kŏr** to express a preference.

ao núm sôm **dee gwàh**	I'd rather have orange juice (literally 'I'd like orange juice better')
ao gài **dee gwàh**	I'd prefer chicken

The comparative

The word **gwàh** is also used after an adjective to make the comparative form:

pairng	expensive	pairng gwàh	more expensive
a-ròy	tasty	a-ròy gwàh	tastier
glai	far	glai gwàh	further

gôr . . .

You will hear Thais use the word **gôr** very frequently. Sometimes it means 'so', or 'therefore', sometimes it means 'too' and sometimes it is simply a *hesitation device* – a sound indicating to the listener that the speaker is still preparing his response, rather like the English, 'Well . . .', or 'Er . . .' If you listen to the dialogue on the tape you will hear Somchai's use of **gôr** as a hesitation device as he ponders over the menu while the waiter hovers, ready to write down the order.

... gôr...

Have you ever . . . ?

ker-ee basically means 'ever' or 'used to' and is placed before verbs to indicate that the action of the verb has occurred at least once in the past. Here are some examples of the way it is used:

ker-ee tahn ah-hăhn tai mái?   *Have (you) ever eaten Thai food?*
ker-ee bpai têe-o chee-ung mài mái?   *Have (you) ever been to Chiangmai?*

To answer 'yes' to questions using **ker-ee**, you simply say **ker-ee** and for 'no' answers, you say **mái ker-ee**.

Not very much (mâi kôy . . . tâo-rài)

mâi kôy . . . is a useful expression meaning 'hardly', 'scarcely', 'not very'. It can be used for toning down negative reactions.
mâi kôy chôrp (tâo-rài)   I don't like it very much
mâi kôy dee (tâo-rài)   It's not very good
mâi-kôy pairng (tâo-rài)   It's not very expensive

things to do

3 If you go out for a meal with a Thai you will almost certainly be asked some of these questions. How would you respond? Be positive!
   1 tahn ah-hăhn tai bpen mái?
   2 chôrp ah-hăhn tai mái?
   3 tahn pèt bpen mái?
   4 a-ròy mái?

4 You've taken some western friends out to a restaurant and they have left you to do the ordering. How would you order
   chicken curry
   beef fried with chillies
   deep-fried omelette
   shrimp 'tom yum'
   and rice?

TRAVELLING AROUND

Transport   Travel outside Bangkok is easy and cheap. There are railway lines running to the north, the north-east, the east and south while regular tour bus services link the capital to major provincial towns. Car hire is probably not advisable – one look at the traffic when you step outside the airport will tell you why! However, if you do need to hire a car for any reason there are sufficient car hire firms in Bangkok whose staff will almost certainly speak English.

Probably the best way to travel around Thailand is by air-conditioned tour bus (**rót too-a**). The services are frequent, cheap, comfortable, and fast. Refreshments are served en route and on longer journeys, a simple meal is usually provided at a regular stopping-off point. (Remember to keep your bus ticket to show in the canteen.) Often the bus will be equipped with a television, too. If you can travel during the day rather than overnight, the journey offers an excellent opportunity to view different landscapes in comfort.

Tour buses are operated both by private companies and by the state-owned Mass Transport Organisation (MTO). Advance booking is nearly always necessary whichever sector you use. Private companies will usually have an office in the centre of Bangkok and English-speaking staff. The MTO buses (called **rót bor kŏr sŏr** – **bor kŏr sŏr** is the Thai acronymn) can be booked from the Northern, Eastern or Southern Bus Terminals, where it is useful to be able to speak Thai.

têe sa-tăhn-nee rót may/at the bus station

Jill and Frank want to visit Chantaburi in the east of Thailand. First they have to find the right booking office for their destination.

Jill: kŏr-tôht kâ   bpai jun-ta-bOO-ree jorng dtŏo-a têe-nǎi?
          Excuse me, please. Where do I book a ticket to Chantaburi?
Thai: têe-nôhn krúp
          Over there.

Jill: kòrp-kOOn kâ . . .   kǒr-tôht kâ   rót bpai jun-ta-bOO-ree òrk **gèe mohng**?
*Thank you . . . Excuse me, please. **What time** does the Chantaburi bus leave?*

Clerk: òrk sèe mohng cháo
One leaves at 10 a.m.

Jill: chái way-lah gèe chôo-a mohng?
How many hours does it take?

Clerk: hâh chôo-a mohng kâ   tĕung jun-ta-bOO-ree bài sǎhm mohng láir òrk bài mohng tĕung hòk mohng yen
Five hours, arriving in Chantaburi at 3 p.m. and another leaves at 1 p.m. arriving at 6 p.m.

Jill: dtǒo-a bai la tâo-rài?
How much is the ticket?

Clerk: bai la róy-hâh-sìp bàht   ja bpai mêu-rai ká?
150 baht. When are you going?

Jill: **kít ja bpai** prÔOng née cháo
***We're thinking of going** tomorrow morning.*

Clerk: prÔOng née cháo dtem láir-o   bài wun née dâi mái?
Tomorrow morning is already full. How about this afternoon?

Jill: dĕe-o dtôrng kít gòrn . . . dâi   ao sǒrng bai
Let me think a minute . . . Yes. Can I have two tickets?

Clerk: nêe kâ   kêun rót têe-nôhn ná kâ
Here you are. You get on the bus over there.

Travelling round Thailand

têe jum-nài dtǒo-a	ticket office
kǒr séu dtǒo-a bpai . . .	I'd like to buy a ticket to . . .
kǒr jorng têe nûng	I'd like to reserve a seat
ja bpai mêu-rài?	When are you going?
òrk	to leave
tĕung	to arrive
dtǒo-a bpai	single ticket

dtŏo-a bpai glùp	return ticket
rót	car
rót may	bus
rót fai	train
reu-a	boat
chahn chah-lah	platform
chún nèung	first class
chún sŏrng	second class
chún săhm	third class
pôo doy-ee săhn	passenger

the way it works

Future tense

As you know, Thai verbs have only one form which can indicate present, past or future time. Sometimes, however, it is necessary to be more specific, in which case a time-marker word is used with the verb. To indicate future time, the word **ja** is used immediately before the main verb:

kít *ja* bpai prÔOng née cháo	We're thinking of going tomorrow morning
chún *ja* séu têe chee-ung mài	I'll buy it in Chiangmai
káo *ja* mah prÔOng née	He'll come tomorrow

Use of classifiers

The classifier for **dtŏo-a** (ticket) is **bai**. Notice that the noun is omitted in the dialogue and the classifier used on its own, where repetition of the noun would have sounded long-winded (*bai* la róy-hâh-sìp . . . and **ao sŏrng** *bai* . . .).

things to do

5.1   You are at the Northern Bus Station in Bangkok, and want to book a ticket for Chiangmai. How would you ask:
1   where to book a ticket for Chiangmai?
2   how much the ticket costs?
3   what time the bus leaves?
4   what time the bus arrives in Chiangmai?
5   where you get on the bus?

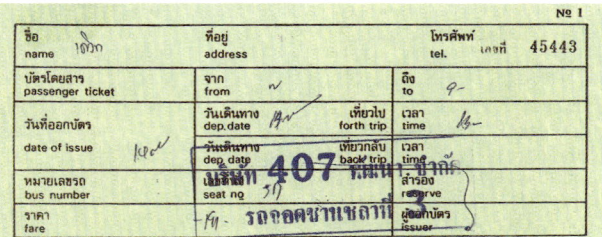

ASKING AND TELLING THE TIME

gèe mohng láir-o?/what's the time?

Frank and Jill return that afternoon to catch the bus. Having got caught up in the Bangkok traffic, they're a bit late:

Frank:	rót bpai jun-ta-bOO-ree òrk gèe mohng krúp?
	What time does the Chantaburi bus leave?
Clerk:	bài mohng krúp
	At 1 p.m.
Frank:	dĕe-o née gèe mohng láir-o?
	What time is it now?
Clerk:	gèu-up bài mohng
	Almost 1 p.m.
Frank:	oo-hoh dtôrng rêep rót òrk jàr.k têe-nǎi?
	Oh dear! We'll have to hurry. Where does the bus leave from?
Clerk:	têe-nôhn krúp
	Over there.

Asking the time

If you want to know what time something happens, use **. . . gèe mohng?** but to ask what time it is, you say **gèe mohng láir-o?** The word **mohng** refers to 'o'clock' hours rather than a stretch of time; if you want to know how many hours something takes, then the word for 'hour' is **chôo-a mohng.**

chái way-lah gèe chôo-a mohng?	How long does it take?
ja yòo gèe chôo-a mohng?	How many hours will (you) be here?

USEFUL WORDS AND PHRASES

cháh	late
ray-o	early
rao dtôrng rêep	We'll have to hurry
mâi dtôrng rêep	There's no need to hurry
bpèrt	open
bpìt	close(d)
pí-pít-ta-pun bpèrt gèe mohng?	What time does the museum open?
ta-na-kahn bpìt gèe mohng?	What time does the bank close?

the way it works

Telling the time

The Thai system of telling the time is very different from our own. The day is divided into four sections of six hours, whereby 7 a.m. and 7 p.m. both become 'one o'clock', 8 a.m. and 8 p.m. 'two o'clock' and so on. In telling the time, a specific word is used to distinguish each of these four periods of the day.

dtee	1 a.m. – 6 a.m.		bài	1 p.m. – approx. 4 p.m.
			yen	4 p.m. – 6 p.m.
cháo	7 a.m. – midday		tÔOm	7 p.m. – midnight

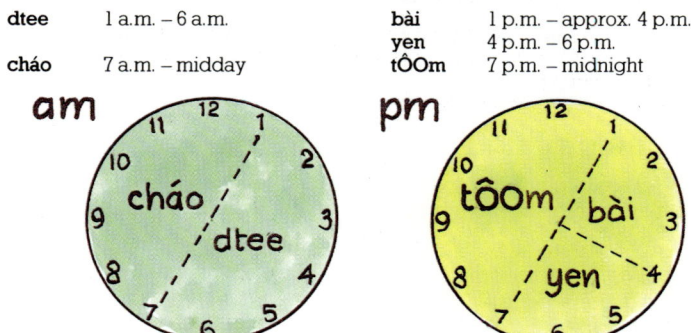

(Notice that the third six-hour period is subdivided into **bài** and **yen**.)

This is how the hours of the day are expressed:

1 a.m.	*dtee* nèung		1 p.m.	*bài* mohng
2 a.m.	*dtee* sŏrng		2 p.m.	*bài* sŏrng *mohng*
3 a.m.	*dtee* săhm		3 p.m.	*bài* săhm *mohng*
4 a.m.	*dtee* sèe		4 p.m.	*bài* sèe *mohng*
5 a.m.	*dtee* hâh		5 p.m.	hâh *mohng yen*
6 a.m.	*dtee* hòk/hòk *mohng cháo*		6 p.m.	hòk *mohng yen*
7 a.m.	*mohng cháo*		7 p.m.	*tÔOm* nèung
8 a.m.	sŏrng *mohng cháo*		8 p.m.	sŏrng *tÔOm*
9 a.m.	săhm *mohng cháo*		9 p.m.	săhm *tÔOm*
10 a.m.	sèe *mohng cháo*		10 p.m.	sèe *tÔOm*
11 a.m.	hâh *mohng cháo*		11 p.m.	hâh *tÔOm*
midday	têe-ung (wun)		midnight	têe-ung keun

(Note that **dtee** and **bài** appear before the number. **dtee** and **tÔOm** do not occur with **mohng**)

The hours from 7 a.m. to 11 a.m. can also be expressed as **jèt mohng cháo**, **bpàirt mohng cháo**, **gâo mohng cháo** and so on.

Half-past the hour is expressed by adding the word **krêung** (half) to the hour time. For the hours from 7 a.m. to 11 a.m. the word **cháo** is usually omitted.

2.30 a.m.	**dtee sŏrng *krêung***	3.30 p.m.	**bài sǎhm mohng *krêung***
8.30 a.m.	**sŏrng mohng *krêung***	5.30 p.m.	**hâh mohng yen *krêung***
11.30 a.m.	**hâh mohng *krêung***	11.30 p.m.	**hâh tÔOm *krêung***

There is no special word for 'quarter past' or 'quarter to' the hour. Minutes past the hour are expressed as: *hour-time* + *number of minutes* + **nah-tee** *(minutes)*

- 10.15 a.m.   **sèe mohng sìp-hâh *nah-tee***
- 2.10 p.m.   **bài sŏrng mohng sìp *nah-tee***
- 9.15 p.m.   **sǎhm tÔOm sìp-hâh *nah-tee***

Minutes to the hour are expressed as:
èek *(further, more)* + *number of minutes to the hour* + *hour time*

- 9.45 a.m.   ***èek* sip-hâh nah-tee sèe mohng cháo** (literally 'fifteen minutes more [to] ten')
- 4.40 p.m.   ***èek* yêe-sìp nah-tee hâh mohng yen**
- 11.50 p.m.   ***èek* sìp nah-tee têe-ung keun**

In the twenty-four hour clock system the word **nah-li-gah** (which can also mean clock/watch) is used for 'hour' and half-hours are expressed as 'thirty minutes past':

- 20.00   **yêe-sìp *nah-li-gah***
- 22.30   **yêe-sìp-sŏrng *nah-li-gah* sǎhm-sìp nah-tee**

things to do

2 Can you match up the times with the right clocks?

dtee sŏrng
èek hâh nah-tee hòk mohng yen
bài sŏrng mohng yêe-sìp-hâh nah-tee

têe-ung krêung
sŏrng tÔOm sìp nah-tee
sǎhm mohng krêung

3 Janya asks you what time it is? Can you tell her?

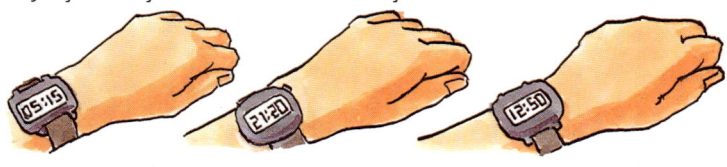

1   2   3

BOOKING A HOTEL ROOM

▶ ▶ ▶ **Hotels**   Staff in Bangkok hotels will, almost without exception, be able to speak English. Since their jobs often depend upon their competence in the language it is best to carry out transactions in English; that way they are spared the embarrassment of perhaps not understanding your Thai and, possibly, appearing to colleagues or superiors, to be inadequate in their command of English. However, if you stay in a small provincial hotel, you might well have to use Thai to book your room. While there is usually someone who can speak English, they are not always around.

Hotel rooms may be air-conditioned (**hôrng air**) or they may have an electric fan on the ceiling (**hôrng tum-ma-dah**); the room includes either a double bed (which Thais describe in English as a 'single room') or two single beds (which in Thailand is a 'double room') and a bathroom. This invariably has a western-style toilet, wash-basin and a bath, shower or traditional water-jar with a small bowl for Thai-style bathing. Use the bowl to scoop up water from the jar and then pour it over yourself. Don't worry about the tiled floor getting wet, or the bedroom flooding: there is a hole for the water to drain out of!

An important thing to check when booking a provincial hotel room is the state of the mesh screens (**mÓOng lôo-ut**) on the windows used to prevent mosquitoes (**yOOng**) getting in. Mosquitoes tend to congregate in bathrooms, particularly near the water jar, and while the hotel staff probably spray the room at least once a day with insecticide (**yah gun yOOng**), it is advisable to be equipped with your own spray, lest any mosquitoes emerge from nowhere to feast on you in the middle of the night.

It is perhaps worth pointing out that many cheap hotels double as brothels and even many of the cheaper 'straight' hotels are used primarily for *liaisons amoureuses*. So if you are greeted by a puzzled look when you arrive alone and ask for a room for a week, you have probably chosen the wrong hotel! The Thai Tourist Authority provides lists of reasonably priced hotels both in Bangkok and up-country.

Hotel prices do not include meals. Often there is a coffee shop in the hotel where you can order both Thai and western food. If it is a large hotel, it may have a number of restaurants, too.

Large hotels will provide information about laundry (and everything else) in English; in smaller hotels you may make an arrangement with the lady who cleans your room. Often, however, hotel laundry services will not accept underwear; these garments can be easily washed yourself in the bathroom.

têe rohng rairm/at the hotel

Frank and Jill have arrived in Chantaburi and are booking a room in a small hotel:

Frank: **mee hôrng wâhng mái** krúp?
         Do you have any free rooms?
Clerk: mee krúp   mee **túng** hôrng air   **láir** hôrng tum-ma-dah
         *Yes. We have **both** air-conditioned rooms **and** ordinary rooms.*

Frank:	**kâh hôrng wun la tâo-rài** krúp?
	What's the daily rate?
Clerk:	hôrng air wun la sǒrng-róy hôrng tum-ma-dah gôr bpàirt-sìp bàht krúp **yòo gèe wun krúp?**
	*Air-conditioned rooms are 200 baht per day. Ordinary rooms are 80 baht. **How long will you be staying?***
Frank:	yung mâi **sâhp** krúp kǒr doo hôrng air gòrn dâi mái?
	*I don't **know** yet. **Could I see the air-conditioned room?***
Clerk:	dâi krúp chern tahng née krúp
	Yes. Please come this way.

Before going out for the evening Frank asks if he can leave some valuables in the hotel safe:

Frank:	kǒr-tôht krúp kǒr fàhk gra-bpǎo kǒrng pǒm têe-nêe dâi mái?
	Excuse me. Can I leave my bag here?
Clerk:	dâi krúp fàhk têe-nêe bplòrt-pai krúp pǒm ja gèp wái nai dtôo sáyf
	Yes, certainly. It's safe to leave them here. I'll keep them in the safe.
Frank:	kòrp-kOOn krúp
	Thank you.
Clerk:	ja bpai têe-o têe-nǎi krúp?
	Where are you going?
Frank:	bpai tahn ah-hǎhn
	We're going to eat.

Booking into a hotel

rohng rairm	hotel
mee hôrng wâhng mái?	Do you have any rooms?
mâi mee hôrng wâhng	We have no rooms/vacancies

ao . . .	I'd like . . .
. . . hôrng air	. . . an air-conditioned room
. . . hôrng dèe-o dtìt air	. . . a single air-conditioned room
. . . hôrng kôo dtìt air	. . . an air-conditioned room with twin beds
. . . hôrng dèe-o tum-ma-dah	. . . an ordinary single room
. . . hôrng kôo tum-ma-dah	. . . an ordinary room with twin beds
núm rórn	hot water
(kít) ja yòo săhm wun	I'm (thinking of) staying three days
kâh hôrng wun la tâo-rài?	How much is the room per day?
hôrng dtìt air rěu bplào?	Does the room have air-conditioning?
tòok gwàh née mee mái?	Do you have anything cheaper?
kŏr doo hôrng gòrn dâi mái?	Could I see the room first, please?
hôrng sŏo-ay mâhk	It's a very nice room
kŏr doo hôrng èun dâi mái?	Could I see another room, please?
kŏr bplèe-un hôrng dâi mái?	Could I change rooms, please?
krêu-ung air *sěe-a*	The air-conditioner is *broken*
pút lom sěe-a	The fan is broken
mÓÓng lôo-ut sěe-a	The screen is broken
chôo-ay *chèet* yah gun yOOng hâi nòy dâi mái?	Can you *spray* some insecticide for me please?
chôo-ay *gâir* hâi nòy dâi mái?	Can you *mend* it for me please?
kŏr náhm gin kòo-ut (nèung)	Could I have a bottle of drinking water?
kŏr bin krúp/kâ	Could we have our bill?

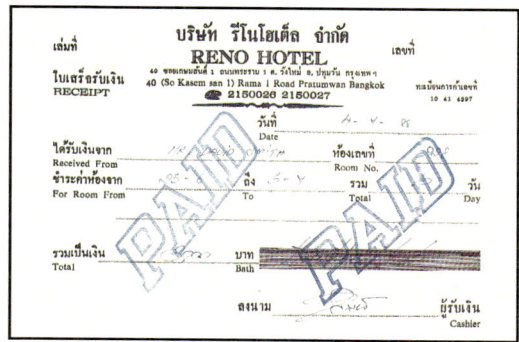

Depositing valuables

kŏr fàhk . . .	Can I leave . . . ?
kŏr fàhk *kŏrng* têe-nêe dâi mái?	Can I leave my *things* here?

. . . núng-sĕu dern tahng	. . . (my) passport
. . . ngern	. . . (my) money
. . . gra-bpǎo	. . .(my) bag(s)
. . . glôrng tài rôop	. . . (my) camera
. . . gOOn-jair	. . . (my) key
bplòrt-pai mái?	Is it safe?
fàhk . . . têe-nêe bplòrt-pai mái?	Is it safe to leave . . . here?

the way it works

The possessive

The possessive is formed using the word **kǒrng** (of).

gra-bpǎo kǒrng pǒm	my bag (literally 'bag of me')
rót kǒrng kOOn	your car
pun-ra-yah kǒrng kOOn Sǒm-chai	Somchai's wife

However it is also quite natural to omit the word **kǒrng** and simply say **gra-bpǎo pǒm**, **rót kOOn** and **pun-ra-yah kOOn Sǒm-chai**.

As you may have noticed from the dialogues, **kǒrng** can also be a noun meaning 'things' or 'possessions'. In the sentence below you can see both uses of the word; the first **kǒrng** is the noun and the second indicates the possessive:

kǒr fàhk kǒrng kǒrng pǒm dâi mái?	Can I leave my things here?

Choosing the right word

sâhp is a polite, rather formal word meaning 'know'; a more informal word with the same meaning is **róo** (cf. **tahn** and **gin** 'eat'). Be careful not to confuse **sâhp** and **róo** with **róo-jùk**: **sâhp** and **róo** are used for knowing facts whereas **róo-jùk** is used for knowing people and places.

things to do

5.4 Imagine you have just arrived at a provincial hotel. Can you book a room?
  1 Receptionist: sa-wùt dee kâ
    [Ask if there are any free rooms]
  2 Receptionist: mee kâ   mee túng hôrng air láir hôrng tum-ma-dah
    [Say you'd like a single room with air-conditioning and ask how much it costs]
  3 Receptionist: hôrng air wun la sǒrng-róy-yêe-sìp bàht
    [Ask if you can see the room]

5.5 Here are some questions you might be asked when booking a room up-country: what do they mean?
  1 ao hôrng tum-ma-dah rĕu hôrng air krúp?
  2 kít ja yòo gèe wun ká?
  3 chêu a-rai krúp?
  4 bpen kon bpra-tâyt a-rai ká?
  5 kǒr doo núng-sĕu dern tahng nòy

AT THE POST OFFICE

Post offices   In Thailand, post offices are open between 8.30 a.m. and 4.30 p.m. on weekdays but are closed at weekends. The Central Post Office on Bangkok's New Road does however open on both Saturday and Sunday mornings. Besides normal post office services, it also offers a 24-hour telegram service and a parcel-packing service. Many of the larger hotels in Bangkok offer post office facilities on the premises.

sòng jòt-măi/sending letters

Frank and Jill want to send a package back to England and get some stamps for postcards:

Frank: nêe sòng bpai ung-grìt tâo-rài krúp?
How much is this to England?

Clerk: sòng bpai tahng ah-gàht rĕu tahng reu-a krúp?
Do you want to send it by air or sea?

Frank: kít wâh sòng bpai tahng reu-a krúp
I think that I'll send it by sea.

Clerk: long ta-bee-un rĕu bplào?
Do you want to register it?

Frank: mâi dtôrng
There's no need.

Clerk: yung ngún gôr bpàirt-sìp-hâh bàht krúp
In that case it'll be 85 baht.

Frank: láir-o sòng póht-gáht bpai ung-grìt tâo-rài krúp?
And how much are postcards to England?

Clerk: bpàirt bàht krúp
Eight baht.

Frank: ao hòk doo-ung krúp   **túng mòt** tâo-rài?
          *I'll have six. How much **altogether**?*
Clerk: róy-sèe-sìp-sǎhm bàht krúp
          A hundred and forty three baht.

At the post office

bprai-sa-nee	post office
póht-gáht	postcard
jòt-mǎi	letter
jòt-mǎi ah-gàht	aerogramme
sa-dtairm	stamp
dtôo bprai-sa-nee	letter box
sòng bpai ung-grìt tâo-rài?	How much is (this) to England?
sòng póht-gáht bpai ung-grìt tâo-rài?	How much is a postcard to England?
sòng bpai tahng ah-gàht	I'll send it by air
sòng bpai tahng reu-a	I'll send it by sea
yàhk ja long ta-bee-un	I want to register it
yàhk ja sòng dòo-un	I want to send it express
yàhk ja sòng dòo-un láir long ta-bee-un	I want to send it express and register it

dtôrng-gahn sòng toh-ra-lâyk (bpai ung-grìt)	I need to send a telegram (to England)
kǒr jòt-mǎi ah-gàht (pàirn nèung)	I'd like an aerogramme
kǒr jòt-mǎi ah-gàht sǎhm pàirn	I'd like three aerogrammes
kǒr sa-dtairm gâo bàht hâh doo-ung	I'd like five 9-baht stamps

SHOPPING

► **Shops**   With traditional markets and pavement stalls existing side by side with multi-storeyed, air-conditioned shopping arcades, Bangkok offers plenty of variety in its shopping facilities. Shops and department stores frequently remain open until 7 or 8 p.m. Usually, their prices are fixed and, unlike markets, bargaining is inappropriate.

séu rorng táo/buying shoes

Jill is browsing in a department store. A pair of shoes catches her eye:

Assistant:	séu a-rai ká?
	Can I help you?
Jill:	**kŏr doo** rorng táo kôo nún dâi mái?
	Can I see *that pair of shoes?*
Assistant:	dâi kâ nêe kâ **lorng sài doo si** ká
	Yes. Here you are. ***Try them on***.
Jill:	kòrp-kOOn kâ lék bpai nòy yài gwàh née mee mái?
	Thank you. They're a bit too small. Do you have anything bigger?

Assistant:	mee kâ **sài ber a-rai** ká?
	*Yes. **What size do you take?***
Jill:	ber hâh kâ
	Size 5.
Assistant:	chôrp sěe a-rai ká? mee sěe dum sěe núm dtahn láir-o gôr sěe kǎo
	Which colour do you like? We've got black, brown and white.
Jill:	kǒr lorng sài sěe kǎo dâi mái?
	Can I try the white?
Assistant:	bpen yung-ngai? sài dâi mái?
	How are they? Can you wear them?

Shopping

hâhng	shop, department store
kǒr doo . . . dâi mái?	Can I see . . . ?
gum-lung doo tâo-nún	I'm just looking
sài ber a-rai?	What size do you take?
chôrp sěe a-rai?	Which colour do you like?
kǒr lorng sài dâi mái?	May I try it on?
yài/lék gern bpai	It's too big/small
yào/sûn gern bpai	It's too long/short
chôo-ay hòr hâi nòy dâi mái?	Could you wrap it up for me please?
rorng táo	shoes
sêu-a	shirt
sêu-a pôo-yǐng	blouse
gra-bprohng	skirt
chái bùt kray-dìt dâi mái?	Can I pay by credit card?

the way it works

More classifiers (doo-ung, pàirn *and* kôo)

The classifier for stamps is **doo-ung**. In the first dialogue Frank omits the word **sa-dtairm** because it is quite clear from the context what he is trying to purchase. For aerogrammes, the classifier is **pàirn**. In the second dialogue, **kôo** which means 'pair' is also the classifier for counting pairs of shoes (**rorng táo sǒrng kôo** two pairs of shoes).

This one, that one

this/these	**née**
that/those	**nún**
that/those (one/s over there)	**nóhn**

When you want to use 'this' or 'that' with a noun, it is normal to use the classifier too:

sa-dtairm doo-ung née   these stamps
gah-fair tôo-ay nún   that cup of coffee
dtum-ròo-ut kon nóhn   that policeman (over there)

You will be relieved to know that if you don't know the right classifier you can use the general classifier **un** (to rhyme with 'fun'). Very often in shops you will hear Thais say **kŏr doo un née** (Can I see this one?) or **ao un nún** (I want that one).

Colours

sĕe is both the noun 'colour' and the verb 'to be a colour'; it occurs in front of all the different colour words. (You can find a list of colours in the English-Thai topic vocabularies on p. 85.)

chôrp **sĕe** a-rai?   Which **colour** do you like?
sĕe dairng   Red.

things to do

1   At the post office, how would you:
    1   ask how much it costs to send a postcard to America?
    2   ask for four 8-baht stamps?
    3   ask for two aerogrammes?
    4   ask to send something by registered mail?

2   Ask the shop assistant if you can have a look at each of the items below. The classifier is given in brackets.
    1   this pair of shoes (**kôo**)
    2   that shirt (**dtoo-a**)
    3   that skirt over there (**dtoo-a**)
    4   this watch (use **un**)

3   True or false?
    1   Frank chôrp sêu-a sĕe dairng
    2   yài gern bpai
    3   Jill séu nah-li-gah
    4   sûn gern bpai

HAVING CLOTHES MADE

Tailors and dressmakers   Clothes can be individually tailored quickly and at very reasonable prices in Thailand. Dressmakers and tailors along Bangkok's Sukhumwit Road and Suriwong Road have traditionally catered for the expatriate community with extensive stocks of material and English-speaking staff. While off-the-peg clothes are becoming increasingly popular, many Thais still prefer to buy their own material from a market that specialises in cloth (like Pahurat Market in Bangkok) and take it to be made up by a dressmaker or tailor. Many operate on a small scale from home or a tiny shop, yet will produce excellent reproductions of designs that customers select from fashion catalogues; and when zips break, buttons come off and holes appear in pockets, they will usually remedy the problem quickly and cheaply.

têe ráhn dtùt sêu-a/at the dressmaker's

Jill wants to have a dress made like one she already has. She takes it to a small dressmaker's shop.

Jill:	dtùt sêu-a chÓOt **yàhng née** dâi mái ká?
	*Can you make a dress **like this**?*
Dressmaker:	ao yàhng née châi mái ká?
	You want it like this, right?
Jill:	châi kâ ao **měu-un gun ler-ee**
	*Yes. I want it **just the same**.*
Dressmaker:	dâi kâ **ao** pâh **mah** dôo-ay rěu bplào?
	*Did you **bring** the material with you?*
Jill:	kâ nêe kâ
	Yes. Here it is.

70

Dressmaker:	sĕe sŏo-ay jung ler-ee **dtômg-gahn mêu-rai?**
	The colour is really lovely. ***When do you want it?***
Jill:	prÔOng née dâi mái ká?
	Can you do it by tomorrow?
Dressmaker:	prÔOng née **kong** mâi sèt kà mah rúp wun ung-kahn yen yen **àht ja** dee gwàh
	*I **probably** won't be finished by tomorrow. It **might** be better to pick it up on Tuesday evening.*
Jill:	mâi dâi kâ prÔOng née glùp bpai ung-grìt prÔOng née bài dâi mái?
	I can't. I'm going back to England tomorrow. How about tomorrow afternoon?
Dressmaker:	oh kay kong dâi kâ bài sãhm mohng ná ká?
	O.K. I probably can. 3 p.m. right?
Jill:	ja kít tâo-rài ká?
	How much will you charge?
Dressmaker:	kít sŏrng-róy bàht kâ mâi pairng kâ
	I'll make it 200 baht. That's not expensive.
Jill:	kâ
	Yes, O.K.

Having clothes made

dtùt sêu-a	to make clothes/have clothes made
dtùt	to cut
yàhk ja dtùt sêu-a	I'd like to have a shirt made
kŏr doo bàirp nòy dâi mái?	Can I see some patterns?

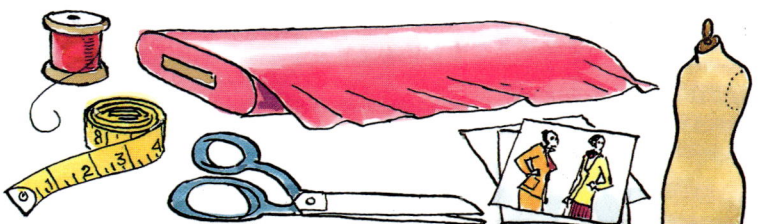

dtùt yàhng née dâi mái?	Can you make it(one) like this?
ao mĕu-un gun ler-ee	I want it just the same
ao sĕe dee-o gun	I want the same colour
mee sĕe a-rai bâhng?	What colours do you have?
mee sĕe èun mái?	Do you have any other colours?
máyt la tâo-rài?	How much per metre?
ao săhm máyt	I want three metres
ja sèt mêu-rai?	When will it be ready?
ja mah rúp dâi mêu-rai?	When can I pick it up?
mah rúp prÔOng née yen yen dâi mái?	Can I pick it up tomorrow evening?
chôo-ay dtìt síp mài hâi dâi mái?	Could you put a new zip on?
chôo-ay bpà gra-bpăo hâi dâi mái?	Could you patch the pocket?
chôo-ay dtìt gra-dOOm mài hâi dâi mái?	Could you put a new button on?
pâh	cloth
pâh măi (tai)	(Thai) silk
pâh fâi	cotton

the way it works

To bring/to take (ao . . . mah/ao . . . bpai)

As you know, **ao** basically means 'want' or 'I'd like', but when it occurs with the verb **mah** (come) or **bpai** (go) it means 'bring' or 'take' respectively:

káo **ao** núng-sĕu dern tahng **mah** dôo-ay	He *brought* his passport with him.
pŏm ja **ao** glôrng tài rôop **bpai** dôo-ay	I'll *take* my camera with me.

If the noun is omitted the words **mah** or **bpai** follow immediately after **ao**:

káo **ao mah** dôo-ay	He *brought* it with him.
pŏm ja **ao bpai** dôo-ay	I'll *take* it with me.
ja **ao bpai** dôo-ay dâi mái?	Can (I) *take* it with (me)?

ao mah/bpai can only be used with *things*. If you want to 'bring' or 'take' *people*, then you use the word **pah . . . mah/bpai**

káo **pah** pêu-un **bpai** doo nŭng	He *took* his friend to see a film
káo **pah** fairn **mah**	He *brought* his wife
pŏm ja **pah bpai** doo	I'll *take* (you) to see it

Really good (dee ler-ee)

The word **ler-ee** has previously been used for emphasis in negative expressions like **mâi gèng ler-ee** (*No good (at it) at all*). It also occurs in positive sentences both on its own and in the expression . . . **jung ler-ee**:

mĕu-un gun **ler-ee**	*just* the same
dee **ler-ee**	*really* good
sŏo-ay **jung ler-ee**	*really* beautiful
pairng **jung ler-ee**	*really* expensive

Probability & possibility

The probability or possibility of something happening can be expressed by using **kong ja . . .** (sure to, bound to, probably . . .) or **àht ja** (might) in front of the verb.

Note that **ja** is optional, and that in negative sentences **kong (ja)** and **àht (ja)** come before the negative word **mâi**:

kong ja sa-nÒOk

That would be fun

káo **àht ja** mâi mah

He might not come

rao **kong** mâi séu

We probably won't buy it

things to do

.4   How would you ask to have a garment made up like the one in the picture?
1   gahng gayng
2   sêu-a
3   gra-bprohng
4   sêu-a chÓOt

.5   The zip on your trousers has broken. How would you ask a dressmaker:
1   if she could put a new one in?
2   if it would be ready tomorrow evening?
3   how much it would cost?

HEALTH PROBLEMS

Health It is advisable to take out some form of medical insurance since medical expenses in the event of serious injury or illness can be costly. All doctors will be able to speak English; those working in the larger private hospitals in Bangkok will often have spent some years studying and working in American hospitals. In the event of illness, doctors at private clinics and private hospitals will usually see patients at very short notice. For less serious problems medicines can be purchased at pharmacies without prescription.

têe ráhn kǎi yah/at the chemist's

Frank has overdone the fruit and has an upset stomach. He goes to the chemist's for advice.

Frank:	mee **yah gâir** tórng sěe-a mái krúp?
	*Have you got any **medicine for** diarrhoea?*
Assistant:	mee krúp nêe krúp
	Yes. Here you are.
Frank:	kǒr doo nòy **chái yung-ngai?**
	*Could I see, please? **How often do you take it?***
Assistant:	gin wun la sèe **mét lúng** ah-hǎhn láir **gòrn** norn
	*Take four **tablets** a day **after** meals and **before** going to sleep.*

Frank:	dtôrng gin gèe wun krúp?
	How many days do you need to take it?
Assistant:	sǎhm wun kong por
	Three days should be enough.
Frank:	tâh yung-ngún ao sìp-sǒrng mét krúp tâo-rài krúp?
	In that case I'd like twelve tablets. How much is that?
Assistant:	yêe-sìp-sèe bàht
	24 baht.

Describing your symptoms

bpen a-rai?	What's the matter
pǒm (chún) róo-sèuk mâi sa-bai	I feel ill
pǒm (chún) bpen wùt	I've got a cold
. . . bpen kâi	. . . a fever
. . . ai	. . . a cough
. . . bpen pòt	. . . prickly heat
. . . tòok dàirt pǎo	. . . sunburn
. . . bpòo-ut hǒo-a	. . . a head-ache
. . . bpòo-ut tórng	. . . stomach-ache
. . . bpòo-ut fun	. . . tooth-ache
. . . bpòo-ut hǒo	. . . ear-ache
. . . tórng sěe-a	. . . diarrhoea
. . . jèp kor	. . . a sore throat
. . . tòok yOOng gùt	. . . been bitten by a mosquito
. . . tòok mǎh gùt	. . . been bitten by a dog
pǒm (chún) ah-jee-un	I've been vomiting
pǒm (chún) norn mâi lùp	I can't sleep
mâi dtôrng bpen hòo-ung	Don't worry
mâi bpen a-rai mâhk	It's not serious

USEFUL WORDS AND PHRASES

yah	medicine
yah tah	ointment, cream
mee yah gâir . . . mái?	Do you have anything for . . . ?
pǒm (chún) gin pen-ní-seen-lin mâi bpen	I can't take penicillin
mee tórng	I'm pregnant
dtôrng norn púk	You must stay in bed
mǒr	doctor
mǒr fun	dentist
rohng pa-yah-bahn	hospital
ráhn kǎi yah	chemist's
bpai hǎh mǒr dâi têe-nǎi?	Where can I find a doctor?

OTHER EMERGENCIES

▶ ▶ ▶ **Loss and theft** Disappearances of items from a hotel should in the first instance be reported to the hotel manager, and his assistance sought if the police are to be called. If you are unfortunate enough to be the victim of pickpockets or muggers, don't fight back. Go to a police station (**sa-tăhn-nee dtum-ròo-ut**), ask for an English-speaking officer and report the incident slowly and clearly in simple English. He will type out a report of the incident in Thai, a copy of which you will probably have to produce if you are making an insurance claim. Only a tiny minority of foreign visitors to Thailand suffer such unfortunate experiences, often through lack of common sense. If in doubt about leaving valuables in a hotel room, ask the manager for advice, and if necessary, deposit items in the hotel safe. Don't carry all your valuables in a bag that can be easily snatched, or invite unwelcome attention with expensive jewellery.

USEFUL WORDS AND PHRASES

gra-bpăo sa-dtung *hăi*	My wallet *has disappeared/is lost*
sa-tăh-nee dtum-ròo-ut yòo têe-năi?	Where's the police station?
rohng pa-yah-bahn yòo têe-năi?	Where's the hospital?
mee krai pôot pah-săh ung-grìt dâi rěu bplào?	Is there anyone who speaks English?
nah-li-gah *tòok ka-moy-ee*	My watch *has been stolen*
krêu-ung dùp plerng	fire extinguisher
mee OO-bùt-dti-hàyt	There's been an accident

Warnings and cries for help

chôo-ay dôo-ay!	Help!
fai mâi!	Fire!
ka-moy-ee!	Burglars! Thieves!
ra-wung!	Watch out!
dtum-ròo-ut!	Police!

Repairs

nah-li-gah *sěe-a*	My watch *is broken*
sôrm dâi mái?	Can you *repair* it?
ja bpai sôrm dâi têe-năi?	Where can I repair it?

ja chái way-lah sôrm nahn mái?	Will it take long to repair it?
ja sèt mêu-rai?	When will it be ready?
ja ao bpai sôrm hâi nòy dâi mái?	Can you get it repaired for me please?
ja sôrm tâo-rài?	How much will it cost to repair?

things to do

.1 Some guests at your hotel have come down with various minor ailments. You're the only one with any Thai and you accompany them to the chemist's. Can you explain what is wrong with each of them?

1 Tom has a sore throat.
2 Helen has been bitten by a dog.
3 Simon has a stomach-ache and diarrhoea.
4 Claire has a cold.

2 Now you are suffering from prickly-heat and sunburn. Complete the dialogue with the chemist.

1 [Ask if he has anything for prickly heat]
Chemist: mee krúp   nêe krúp
2 [Thank him and tell him you are also suffering from sunburn]
Chemist: gôr . . . mee yah tah krúp
3 [Ask him how long you should use it for]
Chemist: sŏrng wun kong por
4 [Say O.K. you'll take it. Ask how much it is altogether]
Chemist: gâo-sìp-hâh bàht krúp
5 [You missed it! Say 'Pardon?']
Chemist: gâo-sìp-hâh bàht krúp

3 How would you explain that:
1 your passport has disappeared?
2 your camera has disappeared?
3 your radio (**wít-ta-yÓO**) has been stolen?
4 you have lost your wallet?

77

ASKING DIRECTIONS

On their last day, Frank and Jill are meeting Somchai and Janya at a well-known restaurant for a farewell meal. They have managed to get out of their taxi at the wrong place and are now trying to find their bearings. Now that Frank is feeling more confident about his Thai, he decides to ask a passer-by for directions.

bpai . . . bpai tahng nǎi?/how do I get to . . . ?

Frank:	kǒr-tôht krúp **bpai** ráhn ah-hǎhn reu-un kwǔn **bpai tahng nǎi** krúp?
	*Excuse me. **How do I get to** the Reuan Kwan Restaurant?*
Passer-by:	tĕung fai sǔn-yahn láir-o lée-o kwǎh kâo soy yêe-sìp-sǎhm
	When you reach the traffic-lights, turn right into soi 23.
Frank:	glai mái krúp?
	Is it far?
Passer-by:	mâi glai ròrk krúp dern bpai gôr hâh nah-tee
	Not at all. It's five minutes' walk.

USEFUL WORDS AND PHRASES

bpai . . . bpai tahng nǎi?	How do I get to . . . ?
yòo tahng kwǎh	It's on the right
yòo tahng sái	It's on the left
lée-o kwǎh	Turn right
lée-o sái	Turn left
ler-ee bpai èek	Go straight on
dtrong	straight, direct
soy	'soi', lane
kâhm sa-pahn bpai	Cross the bridge
fai sǔn-yahn	traffic-light
sèe yâirk	cross-roads
dern bpai bpra-mahn sìp nah-tee	It's about 10 minutes walk
yòo *dtrong kâhm* ta-na-kahn	It's *opposite* the bank
yòo *sÒOt* soy	It's *at the end of* the sci
yòo bpàhk soy	It's *at the beginning of* the soi
yòo *glâi glâi* pi-pít-ta-pun	It's *near* the museum
yòo *tǎir-o tǎir-o* sa-yǎhm sa-kwair	It's *in the* Siam Square *vicinity*
yòo *kâhng lǔng/kâhng nâh* rohng rairm	It's *behind/in front* of the hotel
yòo *dtìt gùp* wút	It's *next* to the temple
bpai táirk-sêe dee gwàh	It's better to go by taxi

things to do

7.4 You need to go to the post office, the bank and then on to the Sirikun Restaurant. Before setting off for each new destination you ask a passer-by for directions. This is what they say:

1 dern dtrong bpai bpra-mahn sŏrng săhm nah-tee   bprai-sa nee yòo tahng sái   dtrong kâhm rohng rairm yài yài

2 lée-o kwăh kâo ta-nŏn sěe fáh   těung sèe yâirk láir-o lée-o sái   ta-nah-kahn yòo tahng kwăh

3 těung sèe yâirk láir-o lée-o láir-o lée-o sái èek   ráhn ah-hăhn yòo tahng kwăh glâi glâi bor-ri-sùt wee ai pee

Plot your route on map A and find out which number corresponds to each of your destinations.

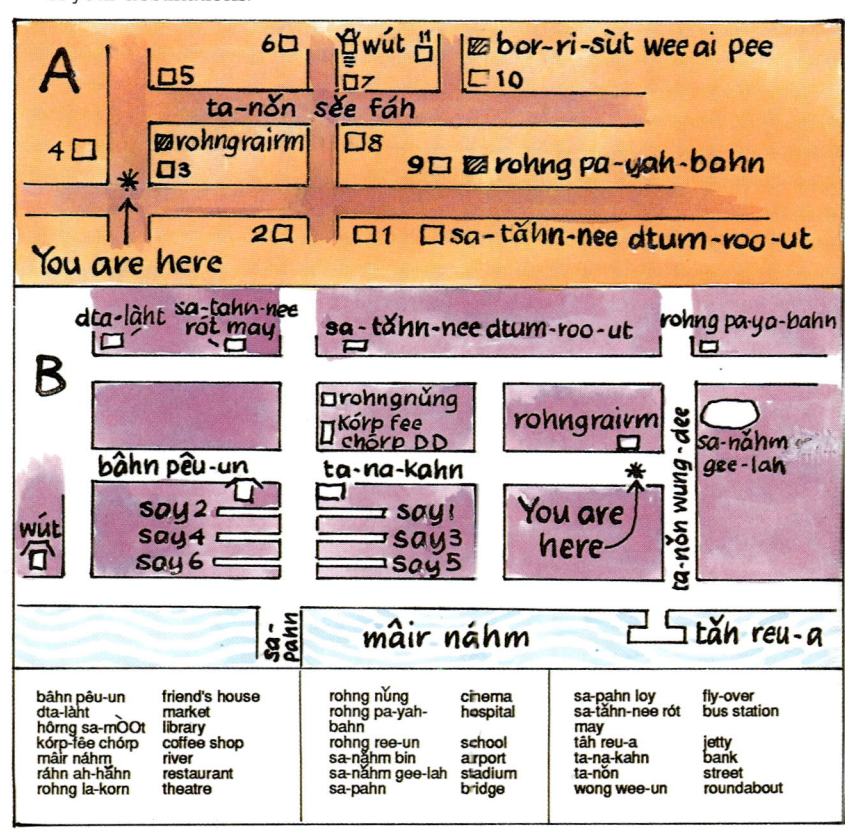

bâhn pêu-un	friend's house	rohng nŭng	cinema	sa-pahn loy	fly-over
dta-làht	market	rohng pa-yah-bahn	hospital	sa-tăhn-nee rót may	bus station
hôrng sa-mŏOt	library				
kórp-lêe chórp	coffee shop	rohng ree-un	school	tăh reu-a	jetty
mâir náhm	river	sa-năhm bin	airport	ta-na-kahn	bank
ráhn ah-hăhn	restaurant	sa-năhm gee-lah	stadium	ta-nŏn	street
rohng la-korn	theatre	sa-pahn	bridge	wong wee-un	roundabout

7.5 Now look at map B. Your taxi-driver is not very familiar with the area. Which of the instructions below would you give him if you wanted to go to:
1 a friend's house on soy 2?
2 the hospital?
3 the DD coffee-shop?

a lée-o sái kâo ta-nǒn wǔng-dee   těung sèe yâirk láir-o lée-o kwǎh   jòrt dtrong kâhm sa-nǎhm gee-lah

b dtrong bpai těung ta-nah-kahn   lée-o kwǎh têe sèe yâirk   yòo dtit gùp rohng nǔng

c dtrong bpai těung ta-nah-kahn   láir-o lée-o sái   jòrt têe bpàhk soy sǒrng

SAYING GOODBYE

Somchai and Janya have driven Jill and Frank to Don Muang airport.

têe sa-nǎhm bin/at the airport

Somchai:	têe-o meu-ung tai sa-nÒOk mái kOOn Jill?
	Did you enjoy your stay in Thailand, Jill?
Jill:	sa-nÒOk mâhk kâ sěe-a jai têe dtôrng rêep glùp
	Yes, it was great. I'm sorry we have to go back so soon.
Janya:	krêu-ung bin těung lorn-dorn gèe mohng ká?
	What time does the plane reach London?
Frank:	bài sèe mohng krúp
	4 p.m.
Somchai:	kǒr hâi dern tahng doy-ee bplòrt-pai ná
	Have a good journey!
Jill:	kòrp-kOOn kâ wun lǔng póp gun mài
	Thank you. See you again sometime.
Frank:	sa-wùt dee krúp
	Goodbye.
Janya:	sa-wùt dee kâ
	Goodbye.
Somchai:	chôhk dee krúp
	Good luck!

USEFUL WORDS AND PHRASES

sa-nǎhm bin	airport
krêu-ung bin	plane
sǑOn-la-gah-gorn	customs
yòo meu-ung tai sa-nÒOk mái?	Have you enjoyed your stay in Thailand?
ah-gàht rórn gern bpai	It's been too hot
sa-nÒOk mâhk	It's been great
tÓOk kon jai dee mâhk	Everyone has been very kind
bpai têe-o têe-nǎi bâhng?	Where did you go/visit?
wun lǔng mah têe-o meu-ung tai èek ná	You must visit Thailand again
yàhk glùp mah têe-o meu-ung tai èek	I'd like to come back to Thailand again
wun lǔng mah têe-o ung-grìt ná	Come to England some time
bpee nâh póp gun mài	See you next year

things to do

7.6 How would you:
1 call for the bill in a restaurant?
2 ask where the post office is?
3 ask how much something costs per kilo?
4 ask what the time the bus leaves?
5 ask a taxi-driver the fare to the airport?
6 respond to an apology?

7.7 What do the following signs mean?

1 ห้ามสูบบุหรี่

2 ญ

หญิง

3 ช

ชาย

4 ระวังสุนัขดุ

1.1 1 kŏr-tôht krúp (kâ) rohng rairm ree-yen yòo têe-nǎi? 2 kŏr-tôht krúp (kâ) rohng nǔng lee-doh yòo têe-nǎi? 3 kŏr-tôht krúp (kâ) hâhng sen-trun yòo têe-nǎi? 4 kŏr-tôht krúp (kâ) wút pra-gâir-o yòo têe-nǎi?
1.2 1 bpai chee-ung mài jorng dtŏo-a têe-nǎi krúp (ká)? 2 bpai chee-ung rai séu dtŏo-a têe-nǎi krúp (ká)? 3 bpai lum-bpahng kêun rót may têe-nǎi krúp (ká)?
1.3 1 Frank: kŏr-tôht krúp gra-bpǎo hǎi   Excuse me. (Our) bags have disappeared.
Chambermaid: gra-bpǎo lěr? yòo têe-nêe kâ   (Your) bags? They're here.
Frank: or . . . kòrp-kOOn krúp kŏr-tôht krúp   Oh . . . Thank you. Sorry.
Chambermaid: mâi bpen rai   That's all right.
1.4 Raise your hand and beckon with your fingers pointing downwards
1 bpai rohng rairm ree-yen tâo-rài? 2 bpai sa-yǎhm sa-kwair tâo-rài? 3 bpai sa-nǎhm bin tâo-rài? 4 bpai sa-nǎhm lǒo-ung tâo-rài?
1.5 1 pairng bpai nòy krúp (kâ) hâh-sìp baht dâi mái? 2 pairng bpai nòy krúp (kâ) jèt-sìp bàht dâi mái? 3 pairng bpai nòy krúp (kâ) hòk-sìp bàht dâi mái? 4 pairng bpai nòy krúp (kâ) sŏrng-róy-hâh-sìp bàht dâi mái? 5 pairng bpai nòy krúp (kâ) sèe-sìp bàht dâi mái?
1.6 1 jòrt dtrong née krúp (kâ) 2 jòrt têe-nôhn krúp (kâ) 3 jòrt tahng kwǎh krúp (kâ) 4 jòrt tahng sái krúp (kâ)

2.1 1 kŏr bee-a sǐng kòo-ut nèung 2 kŏr núm kǎirng bplào gâir-o nèung 3 kŏr koh-lâh sǎhm kòo-ut 4 kŏr gah-fair sŏrng tôo-ay 5 kŏr núm sôm kún hâh gâir-o
2.2 1 c, 2 e, 3 a, 4 b, 5 d.
2.3 nǒo nǒo kŏr bpép-sêe sŏrng kòo-ut núm sôm kún gâir-o nèung lair-o gôr gah-fair tôo-ay nèung
2.4 1 glôo-ay wěe la tâo-rài? 2 sôm loh la tâo-rài? 3 lum-yai loh la tâo-rài? 4 ma-la-gor bai la tâo-rài?
2.5 1 wěe la yêe-sìp-hâh chái mái? lót nòy dâi mái? 2 loh la sèe-sìp chái mái? lót nòy dâi mái? 3 loh la sǎhm-sìp-hâh chái mái? lót nòy dâi mái? 4 bai la sìp-bpàirt chái mái? lót nòy dâi mái?

2.6 1 nêe a-rai krúp (ká)? 2 a-rai ná?
2.7a 1 kŏr pôot gùp kOOn Mah-lee nòy dâi mái krúp (ká)? 2 kŏr dtòr ber sǎhm-hâh-hòk (356) kŏr pôot gùp kOOn Châht-chai nòy dâi mái krúp (ká)? 3 kŏr pôot gùp kOOn Su-ra-chai nòy dâi mái krúp (ká)?
2.7b 1 kOOn Mah-lee yung mâi glùp ja glùp dtorn yen krúp 2 kOOn Châht-chai bpai tOO-rá yung mâi glùp kâ 3 dâi krúp ror děe-o ná krúp
2.8 1 kŏr pôot gùp kOOn Nóy nòy dâi mái krúp (ká)? 2 pǒm/chún . . . bpen pêu-un kOOn Nóy 3 dtorn bài pǒm (chún) toh mah mài kòrp-kOOn krúp (kâ) sa-wùt dee krúp (kâ)

3.1 1 sa-wùt dee krúp (kâ) kOOn Sŏm-chai 2 sa-wùt dee krúp (kâ) kOOn Jun-yah sa-bai dee lěr krúp (ká)? 3 sa-wùt dee krúp (kâ) kOOn Châht-chai bpen yung-ngai bâhng? 4 pǒm (chún) chêu . . . yin dee têe dâi róo-jùk
3.2 1 bpen nít-nòy krúp (kâ) 2 mâi nahn krúp (kâ) 3 chôrp mâhk krúp (kâ)
3.3 1 bpen kon yer-ra-mun krúp 2 bpen kon ung-grìt kâ 3 bpen kon tai kâ 4 bpen kon a-may-ri-gun krúp
3.4 1 mâi gèng ròrk krúp (kâ) 2 mâi chút ròrk krúp (kâ) 3 mâi gèng ròrk krúp (kâ) 4 mâi chút ròrk krúp (kâ)
3.5 These are my parents. My father comes from China but he's lived in Thailand for a long time. He's the manager of a company in Songkhla in the south. My mother is Thai. She comes from the south, from Phuket. She doesn't work; she's a housewife.
3.6 1 nêe krai krúp (ká)? 2 chêu a-rai krúp (ká)? 3 ah-yÓO tâo-rài krúp (ká)? 4 tum ngahn a-rai krúp (ká)?
3.7 1 pǒm (chún) tum ngahn nai orp-fít têe lorn-dorn 2 dtàirng ngahn láir-o 3 mee lôok láir-o pôo-chai kon nèung láir pôo-yǐng kon nèung 4 pôo-chai ah-yÓO sìp kòo-up láir pôo-yǐng ah-yÓO sǎhm kòo-up tâo-nún

4.1 1 See some Thai dancing. 2 Doesn't know where to see it. 3 Suggests a large restaurant as most appropriate place and offers to take Jill to a tour company that arranges such entertainments.

Janya: prÔÔng née kOOn Jill ja bpai
tê-o tê-nǎi?
Where are you going tomorrow
Jill?

Jill: yàhk ja bpai doo rum tai
I'd like to see some Thai
dancing.
dtàir mâi sâhp wâh ja bpai doo
dâi tê-nǎi
But I don't know where I can go
and see it.
tê rohng la-korn hàirng châht
mee mái?
Do they have it at the National
Theatre?

Janya: kít wâh bpai doo tê ráhn ah-
hǎhn dee gwàh
I think it's better to go and see it
at a restaurant.
ráhn ah-hǎhn yài yài mee rai-
gahn rum tai tÓÓk keun
Big restaurants have
programmes of Thai dancing
every night.

Jill: ráhn ah-hǎhn a-rai ká?
Which restaurants?

Janya: gôr . . . mâi sâhp kâ
I don't know.
dtôrng bpai tǎhm tê bor-ri-sùt
num tê-o
We'll have to go and ask at a tour
company.
děe-o ja pah bpai tǎhm doo
In a minute I'll take you there to
inquire.

4.2 1 False, 2 True, 3 True, 4 False
4.3 1 bpen krúp (kâ) 2 chôrp krúp
(kâ) 3 bpen krúp (kâ) 4 a-ròy krúp (kâ)
4.4 kǒr gairng gài néu-a pùt prík kài
jee-o dtôm yum gÔÔng láir-o gôr kâo

5.1 1 bpai chee-ung mài jorng dtǒo-a
tê-nǎi? 2 dtǒo-a bai la tâo-rài? 3 rót
(bpai chee-ung mài) òrk gèe mohng?
4 (rót) těung chee-ung mài gèe mohng?
5 kêun rót may tê-nǎi?
5.2 09.30 = sǎhm mohng krêung;
14.25 = bài sǒrng mohng yêe-sìp-hâh
nah-tee; 20.10 = sǒrng tÔÔm sìp nah-
tee; 17.55 = èek hâh nah-tee hòk
mohng yen; 02.00 = dtee sǒrng;
12.30 = tê-ung krêung
5.3 1 hâh mohng yen sìp-hâh nah-tee

2 sǎhm tÔÔm yêe-sìp nah-tee 3 èek
sìp nah-tee bài mohng
5.4 1 mee hôrng wâhng mái? 2 ao
hôrng dèe-o dtìt air kâh hôrng wun la
tâo-rài? 3 kǒr doo hôrng gòrn dâi mái?
5.5 1 Do you want an ordinary room
or an air-conditioned room? 2 How
many days are you planning on staying?
3 What's your name, please? 4 Which
country do you come from? 5 Could I
see your passport, please?

6.1 1 sòng póht-gáht bpai a-may-ri-
gah tâo-rài? 2 kǒr sa-dtairm bpàirt bàht
sèe doo-ung 3 kǒr jòt-mǎi ah-gàht
sǒrng pàirn 4 kǒr (or yàhk ja) long
ta-bee-un
6.2 1 kǒr doo rorng táo kôo née 2 kǒr
doo sêu-a dtoo-a nún 3 kǒr doo gra-
bprohng dtoo-a nóhn 4 kǒr doo nah-li-
gah un née
6.3 1 False, 2 False, 3 True, 4 False.
6.4 1 dtùt gahng gayng yàhng née dâi
mái krúp (ká)? 2 dtùt sêu-a yàhng née
dâi mái krúp (ká)? 3 dtùt gra-bprohng
yàhng née dâi mái krúp (ká)? 4 dtùt
sêu-a chÓÓt yàhng née dâi mái krúp
(ká)?
6.5 1 chôo-ay dtùt síp mái hâi dâi mái
krúp (ká)? 2 mah rúp prÔÔng née yen
dâi mái krúp (ká)? 3 (ja kít) tâo-rài krúp
(ká)?

7.1 1 Tom jèp kor 2 Helen tòok mǎh
gùt 3 Simon bpòo-ut tórng láir tórng
sěe-a 4 Claire bpen wùt
7.2 1 mee yah gâir pòt mái krúp (ká)?
2 kòrp-kOOn krúp (kâ) pǒm (chún)
tòok dàirt pǎo dôo-ay 3 dtôrng chái gèe
wun? 4 O.K. krúp (kâ) túng mòt tâo-rài
krúp (ká)? 5 a-rai ná?
7.3 1 núng-sěu dern tahng (kǒrng
pǒm/chún) hǎi 2 glôrng tài rôop hǎi
3 wít-ta-yÓÓ tòok ka-moy-ee 4 gra-
bpǎo sa-dtung hǎi
7.4 1 post office = 4 2 bank = 7
3 Sirikun Restaurant = 10
7.5 1 c 2 a 3 b
7.6 1 gèp dtung krúp (kâ) 2 bprai-sa-
nee yòo tê-nǎi? 3 loh la tâo-rài? 4 rót
may òrk gèe mohng? 5 bpai sa-nǎhm
bin tâo-rài? 6 mâi bpen rai krúp (kâ)
7.7 1 No smoking 2 Ladies' toilet
3 Men's toilet 4 Beware of the dog

TOPIC VOCABULARY

Cardinal numbers

1	nèung	11	sìp-et	21	yêe-sìp-èt	31	săhm-sìp-èt
2	sŏrng	12	sìp-sŏrng	22	yêe-sìp-sŏrng	32	săhm-sìp-sŏrng
3	săhm	13	sìp-săhm	23	yêe-sìp-săhm	40	sèe-sìp
4	sèe	14	sìp-sèe	24	yêe-sìp-sèe		etc.
5	hâh	15	sìp-hâh	25	yêe-sìp-hâh	50	hâh-sìp
6	hòk	16	sìp-hòk	26	yêe-sìp-hòk	60	hòk-sìp
7	jèt	17	sìp-jèt	27	yêe-sìp-jèt	70	jèt-sìp
8	bpàirt	18	sìp-bpàirt	28	yêe-sìp-bpàirt	80	bpàirt-sìp
9	gâo	19	sìp-gâo	29	yêe-sìp-gâo	90	gâo-sìp
10	sìp	20	yêe-sìp	30	săhm-sìp	100	(nèung) róy

101	(nèung) róy-nèung	1,000	(nèung) pun
150	(nèung) róy-hâh-sìp	2,000	sŏrng-pun
200	sŏrng-róy	3,500	săhm-pun-hâh-róy
300	săhm-róy	7,924	jèt-pun-gâo-róy-yêe-sìp-sèe
400	sèe-róy	10,000	mèun
500	hâh-róy	100,000	săirn
	etc.	1,000,000	láhn

Ordinal numbers

1st	têe nèung
2nd	têe sŏrng
3rd	têe săhm
4th	têe sèe
5th	têe hâh
	etc.

This is what the numbers 1 to 10 look like in Thai script:

1	๑	5	๕	8	๘
2	๒	6	๖	9	๙
3	๓	7	๗	10	๑๐
4	๔				

Months (deu-un)

January	mók-ga-rah-kom
February	gOOm-pah-pun
March	mee-nah-kom
April	may-săh-yon
May	préut-sa-pah-kom
June	mí-tOO-nah-yon
July	ga-rúk-ga-dah-kom
August	sing-hăh-kom
September	gun-yah-yon
October	dtOO-lah-kom
November	préut-sa-jìk-gah-yon
December	tun-wah-kom

Days (wun)

Monday	wun jun
Tuesday	wun ung-kahn
Wednesday	wun pÓÒt
Thursday	wun pá-réu-hùt
Friday	wun sÒÒk
Saturday	wun săo
Sunday	wun ah-tít
today	wun née
tomorrow	prÔÒng née
yesterday	mêu-a wahn née
weekend	wun săo wun ah-tít

Seasons (nâh)

Cool season	(November – February)	nâh năo
Hot season	(March – June)	nâh rórn
Rainy season	(July – October)	nâh fŏn

Clothes (sêu-a pâh)

belt	kĕm kùt
blouse	sêu-a pôo-yǐng
bra	sêu-a yók song
briefs	gahng gayng nai sa-dtree
dress	sêu-a chÓOt
hat	mòo-uk
jacket	sêu-a nôrk
jeans	gahng gayng yeen
nightdress	chÓOt norn
pyjamas	sêu-a gahng gayng norn
shirt	sêu-a
shoes	rorng táo
shorts	gahng gayng kǎh sûn
skirt	gra-bprohng
socks	tÔOng táo
stockings	tÔOng nôrng
suit (men's)	chÓOt sǎh-gon
swimming costume	chÓOt wâi náhm
t-shirt	sêu-a yêut
tie	nék-tai
trousers	gahng gayng
underpants	gahng gayng nai

Colours (sĕe)

black	sĕe dum
blue	sĕe núm ngern
(light) blue	sĕe fáh
brown	sĕe núm dtahn
green	sĕe kĕe-o
grey	sĕe tao
pink	sĕe chom-poo
red	sĕe dairng
white	sĕe kǎo
yellow	sĕe lĕu-ung
dark	sĕe gàir
dark green	sĕe kĕe-o gàir
light	sĕe òrn
light green	sĕe kĕe-o òrn

The chemist's (ráhn kǎi yah)

aspirin	air-sa-bprin
bandage	pâh pun plǎir
condom	tÔOng yahng
contraceptive pill	yah kOOm gum-nèrt
medicine	yah (náhm)
ointment	yah (tah)
perfume	yah hǒrm
pill	yah (mét)
plaster	bplah-sa-dter
razor	mêet gohn
razor blade	bai mêet gohn
sanitary towels	pâh a-nah-mai
shampoo	yah sà pǒm
shaving soap	sa-bòo gohn nòo-ut
soap	sa-bòo
'tiger balm' ointment	yah mòrng
toothbrush	bprairng sĕe fun
toothpaste	yah sĕe fun

FOOD (ah-hǎhn)

meat (néu-a)

beef	néu-a (woo-a)
chicken	gài
duck	bpèt
pork	mǒo

fish (bplah)

crab	bpoo
lobster	gÔOng gâhm grahm
mussels	hǒy malairng pôo
shellfish	hǒy
shrimp	gÔOng
squid	bplah-mèuk

vegetables (pùk)

bamboo shoots	nòr-mái
beansprouts	tòo-a ngôrk
cabbage	ga-lùm-bplee
cauliflower	dòrk ga-lùm-bplee
chilli	prík
cucumber	dtairng gwah
garlic	gra-tee-um
ginger	king
lettuce	pùk-gàht
'morning glory'	pùk bÔOng
mushroom	hèt
onion	hǒo-a hǒrm
pepper	prík yòo-uk
spring green	pùk ka-náh
spring onion	dtôn hǒrm
sweet corn	kâo pôht
tomato	ma-kĕu-a tâyt

fruit (pǒn-la-mái)

banana	glôo-ay
coconut	ma-práo
custard apple	nóy-nàh
durian	tÓO-ree-un
grape	a-ngÒOn
guava	fa-rùng
jackfruit	ka-nÒOn
lime	ma-nao
longan	lum-yai
lychee	lín-jèe
mango	ma-môo-ung
mangosteen	mung-kÓOt
orange	sôm
papaya	ma-la-gor
pineapple	sùp-bpa-rót
pomelo	sôm oh
rambutan	ngór
rose apple	chom-pôo
sapodilla	la-mÓOt
water melon	dtairng moh

other foodstuffs

bread	ka-nǒm bpung
butter	ner-ee
cheese	ner-ee kǎirng
chilli sauce	núm prík
coffee	gah-fair
fish sauce	núm bplah
milk	nom
noodles	gǒo-ay dtěe-o
pepper	prík tai
rice	kâo
salt	gleu-a
sugar	núm dtahn
tea	chah
vegetable oil	núm mun pêut

cooking terms

baked	òp
barbecued	yâhng
boiled	dtôm
(deep) fried	tôrt
(stir) fried	pùt
toasted	bpîng

eating places

restaurant	ráhn ah-hǎhn
noodle shop	ráhn gǒo-ay dtěe-o
coffee shop	kórp-fêe chórp

Parts of the body

ankle	kôr táo
arm	kǎirn
back	lǔng
chest	òk
ear	hǒo
eye	dtah
face	nâh
finger	néw
foot	táo
hair	pǒm
hand	meu
head	hǒo-a
heart	hǒo-jai
leg	kǎh
mouth	bpàhk
neck	kor
nose	ja-mòok
skin	pěw-nǔng
stomach	tórng

Family and relatives

brother (elder)	pêe-chai
brother (younger)	nórng-chai
brothers and sisters	pêe-nórng
child	dèk
child (one's own)	lôok
father	pôr
grandchild	lǎhn
grandfather (paternal)	bpòo
grandfather (maternal)	yâh
grandmother (paternal)	dtah
grandmother (maternal)	yai
mother	mâir
parents	pôr mâir
sister (elder)	pêe-sǎo
sister (younger)	nórng-sǎo

Workplaces

I work in . . .	pǒm (chún) tum ngahn nai . . .
a bank	ta-nah-kahn
a clinic	klee-nìk
a college	wit-ta-yah-lai
a factory	rohng ngahn
a firm	bor-ri-sùt
a garage	òo sôrm rót
at home	têe bâhn
a hospital	rohng pa-yah-bahn
an office	orp-fìt
a school	rohng ree-un
a shop	ráhn

Occupations

businessman/woman	núk tÓO-rá-gìt	maid	kon chái
civil servant	kâh-râht-cha-gahn	mechanic	chûng krêu-ung
company employee	pa-núk-ngahn bor-ri-sùt	monk	prá
company manager	pôo-jùt-gahn bor-ri-sùt	nurse	pa-yah-bahn
dentist	mŏr fun	policeman	dtum-ròo-ut
doctor	mŏr	photographer	chûng tài rôop
driver	kon kùp rót	secretary	lay-kăh-nÓO-gahn
housewife	mâir bâhn		
journalist	núk núng-sĕu-pim	soldier	ta-hăhn
lawyer	ta-nai kwahm	student	núk sèuk-săh
lecturer	ah-jahn	teacher	kroo

Countries and nationalities

American	a-may-ri-gah; a-may-ri-gun	Japanese	yêe-bpÒOn
Australian	órt-sa-tray-lee-a	Indonesian	in-doh-nee-see-a
British/English	ung-grìt	Lao	lao
Burmese	pa-mâh	Malaysia	ma-lay-see-a
Cambodian	ka-măyn	Russian	rút-see-a
Canadian	kair-nah-dah	Singapore	sĭng-ka-bpoh
Chinese	jeen	Thai	tai
French	fa-rùng-sàyt	Vietnamese	wêe-ut nahm
German	yer-ra-mun		

For countries, the word **bpra-tâyt** (formal) or **meu-ung** (colloquial) normally appears in front of the word given above; for the inhabitants of that country use **kon**; for the language use **pah-săh**:

bpra-tâyt ung-grìt Britain, England
kon tai a Thai person, Thai people
pah-săh yêe-bpÒOn Japanese language

Pronouns

I	**pŏm** (male); **dee-chún/chún** (female)
you (sing./plural)	**kOOn; tûn** (polite form used to superiors and by announcers on T.V. radio etc.)
he, she, they	**káo**
we	**rao**

Classifiers

bai	for some fruits; tickets
kon	for people
kôo	for pairs of things e.g. shoes
mét	for pills
pàirn	for sheets of paper
un	miscellaneous

containers (**tôo-ay, jahn, kòo-ut, gâir-o** etc.)
units of time (**nah-tee, wun, deu-un** etc.)
units of measurement (**loh, máyt** etc.)

ah-gàht weather; air
ah-hǎhn food
ah-tít week
àht (ja) might, may
ah-yǑO age
ai dtǐm ice-cream
air air-conditioned
a-nǑO-sǎh-wa-ree monument
ao want
ao bpai take
a-rai something
a-rai? what?
a-rai gôr dâi anything
a-rai ná? pardon?
a-ròy tasty

bâhn house
bàht baht (*unit of Thai currency*)
báht basketball
bàird-min-dtûn badminton
bàirp pattern
ber number; size
ber toh-ra-sùp telephone number
bin bill
bOO-rèe cigarette
bon on
bòrk say (*v*)
bor-ri-sùt company
bpà patch (*v*)
bpàhk mouth
bpàhk soy beginning of a *soi*
bpai go (*v*)
. . . bpai nòy a bit
bpee year
bpen is, am,are
bpen wùt have a cold
. . . bpen can
bpèrt open (*v, a*)
bpìt close(d) (*v, a*)
bplào no
bplèe-un change (*v*)
bplòrt-pai safe
bporn pound (sterling)
bpra-tâyt country
bprai-sa-nee post office
bùt kray-dìt credit card

cháh slow(ly); late
chahm bowl
chahn chah-lah platform
chái use (*v*)
cháo morning
chee-ung mài Chiangmai
chee-ung rai Chiangrai

chèet spray; inject
chék dern tahng traveller's cheque
chern invite; please
chêu name; be named
chìm taste (*v*)
chôo-ay help (*v*); please
chôo-ay dôo-ay help!
chórn spoon
chôrp like
chún I (*shortened form of* **dee-chún**)
chún nèung, sǒrng, sǎhm first, second,
    third class
chút clear

dâi can
. . . dâi mái? can . . . ?
dee good
dee gwàh better
dee-chún I (*female speaker*)
dee-o single
dǎe-o a moment, a minute
dèk child
doo see
dôo-ay too; with
dòo-un express; urgent
doo-ung *classifier for stamps*
dorn-lâh dollar
dtàir but
dtàirng ngahn marry
dtàirng ngahn láir-o married
dta-làht market
dtem full
dtìt stick, stuck, attach; **rót dtìt** traffic jam
dtó table
dtòk long agree
dtoo-a *classifier for items of clothing*
dtǒo-a ticket
dtóo bprai-sa-nee letter box
dtòr extend
dtòr ber (telephone) extension
dtorn bài afternoon
dtorn cháo morning
dtorn née now
dtorn yen evening
dtôrng have to, must
mâi dtôrng there's no need
dtôrng-gahn want, need
dtǑOk dtǑOk 3-wheeled motorised
    rickshaw
dtrong straight, exact, direct
dtrong née right here
dtum-ròo-ut police(man)
dtung money

VOCABULARY

dtùt cut
dtùt sêu-a make clothes, have clothes made

èek again; further
ee-sǎhn the North-East of Thailand
èun other

fàhk entrust, leave something
fai sǔn-yahn traffic-light
fairn girl-, boy-friend; husband, wife
fa-rùng *farang*, westerner, caucasian
fÓOt-born football

gahng gayng trousers
gâir mend, repair; cure
gâir-o glass
gào old
gâo-êe chair
gèe? how many?
gee-lah sport
gèng to be good at
gèp collect; keep
gèp dtung can I have the bill?
gèp wái keep
... (gern) bpai too ..., too much
gin eat, drink
glahng middle
glai far
glâi near
glôrng tài rôop camera
glùp return
gôr well, um ... (*hesitation device*)
... gôr dâi can
... gôr láir-o gun settle for ...
gòrn before; first; **ah-tít gòrn** last week
gOOn-jair key
gra-bpǎo bag, luggage; wallet; pocket
gra-bpǎo (sa-dtung) wallet
gra-bprohng skirt
gra-dOOm button
grOOng-tâyp Bangkok ('city of angels')
gùp with
gwàh (more) than

há *an informal variant of* **krúp/kâ**
hâi get someone to do something
hǎi disappear; lost
hâhm forbid; 'No ...
hâhng store, department store
hěw náhm thirsty
hôrng room
hôrng dèe-o single room
hôrng kôo double room
hôrng náhm toilet
hôrng sa-mÒOt library

ja will, shall (*future tense marker*)
jàhk from
jahn place
jâo náh-têe official
jeen China, Chinese
jing true
jing jing really
jórk-gîrg jogging
jorng book (*v*)
jòrt park (a car)
jòt-mǎi letter
jòt-mǎi ah-gàht aerogramme
jung-wùt province
jung ler-ee very

kâ/ká *female polite particle*
kâh cost
ka-moy-ee burglar, thief
ka-nǒm cake, sweet, dessert
káo he, she, they
kâo enter
kâo rice (*the vowel sound is longer than in the word for 'enter'*)
kâo dtôm rice 'porridge'
ker-ee used to; have ever ...
kêun get on (a bus)
kít think; calculate
kít wâh ... (I) think that ...
kon person
kong (ja) bound to, sure to
kôo pair
kòo-up years old (*for children*)
kòo-ut bottle
kǒr ask for; can I have ...?
kǒr-tôht excuse me; sorry
kǒrng things; of
kǒrng wǎhn dessert
kòrp-kOOn thank you
kOOn you
krai? who?
krêung half
krêu-ung air air-conditioner
krêu-ung bin plane
krêu-ung dùp plerng fire extinguisher
kroo teacher
krúng time, instance
krúng dee-o once
krúp *male polite particle*
kwǎh right

la per
lah pùk take time off work
lǎi several, many
láir and
láir-o already; and then

89

láir-o gôr and
lée-o turn
lék small
lên play (v)
lěr question word
ler-ee (bpai) go on further
ler-ee: mâi . . . ler-ee not . . . at all
lêrk give up
loh kilo
long ta-bee-un register (v)
lôok (one's own) children
lorng try (something)
lót reduce
lum-bpahng Lampang
lŭng after

mah come
mâhk very, much
mái? question word
mâi not; negative word
mâi . . . ler-ee not . . . at all
mâi . . . ròrk not . . . at all
mâi bpen rai never mind; that's all right
mâi kôy . . . (tâo-rài) not very, hardly
mái kèet match
mǎir! goodness!
mâir mother
mâir bâhn housewife
mâir náhm river
may-noo menu
máyt metre
mee have; there is/are
mêet knife
mét tablet; classifier for pills
mêu-a when (in the past)
mêu-a gòrn in the past, previously
mêu-rai? when?
měu-un gun likewise, similar
meu-ung town; country
meu-ung tai Thailand
mohng hour (clock); **gèe mohng?** what time?
mǒr doctor
mǒr fun dentist
moo-ay boxing
mÓOng lôo-ut window screens

ná particle: O.K.? Right? . . . , you know
nâh rúk lovely, sweet
nah-li-gah hour (24 hr clock); watch, clock
náhm water, drink
nahn a long time
ná-korn-râht-cha see-mah Nakorn Ratchasima (Korat)

nǎi? question word: which? where?
née this, these
nêe a-rai? What is this/are these?
nèu-ay tired
ngahn work
ngern money
ngêe-up quiet, peaceful
nít (nèung) a bit
nít-nòy a bit
nóhn that (over there)
nǒo nǒo waitress!
norn sleep, go to bed
nórng-chai younger brother
nórng-sǎo younger sister
nǒrng-kai Nongkhai
nòy a little
núk sèuk-sǎh student
núk tÓO-rá-gìt businessman/woman
núm mun petrol
nún that
núng-sěu dern tahng passport

òrk leave
OO-bùt-dti-hàyt accident
orp-fít office

pâh cloth
pâh mǎi silk
pâh fâi cotton
pah-sǎh language
pâhk dtâi the South
pàirn classifier for aerogrammes
pairng expensive
pêe-chai elder brother
pêe-nórng brothers and sisters
pêe-sǎo elder sister
pêu-un friend
pèt hot, spicy
pi-pít-ta-pun museum
póht-gáht postcard
pǒm I (male speakers)
pǒn-la-mái fruit
pôo-chai male, man, boy
pôo doy-ee sǎhn passenger
poo-gèt Phuket
pôo-jùt-gahn manager
pôo-yǐng female, woman, girl
pôot speak
por enough
pôr father
prÔOng née tomorrow
púk rest (v)
pút lom fan

ráhn shop

VOCABULARY

ráhn ah-hǎhn restaurant
ráhn gǒo-ay dtěe-o noodle shop
rai-gahn programme
rao we
ra-wung! look out! be careful!
ray-o early
rêe-uk be called
rêe-uk wâh . . . it's called . . .
ree-un study (v)
rěe-un coin
rěu or
. . . rěu bplào? . . . or not?
reu-a boat
rohng la-korn theatre
rohng nǔng cinema
rohng pa-ya-bahn hospital
rohng rairm hotel
rohng ree-un school
róo know (facts)
róo-jùk know (people, places)
róo-sèuk (wâh . . .) feel (that . . .)
ror wait
ròrk: mâi . . . ròrk not . . . at all
rórn hot
rorng táo shoe
rót car; vehicle
rót may bus
rót fai train
rum tai Thai dancing
rúp take; receive; pick up; eat (polite)

sa-bai dee well, fine
sa-dtairm stamp
sǎh-mee husband
sǎhm-lór samlor: 3-wheeled motorised
    rickshaw
sâhp know (facts)
sài wear; put on (clothes); put
sái left
sǎi line (telephone)
sa-nǎhm bin airport
sa-nǎhm gee-lah stadium
sa-nǎhm lǒo-ung Sanam Luang
sa-nǎhm máh race course
sa-nǎhm ten-nít tennis course
sa-nÒOk have fun (v)
sa-pahn bridge
sa-pahn loy fly-over
sa-tǎh-nee dtum-ròo-ut police station
sa-tǎh-nee rót may bus station
sà wâi náhm swimming pool
sa-wùt dee hello; goodbye
sa-yǎhm sa-kwair Siam Square
sěe colour

sěe-a broken
sèe yâirk cross-roads
sèt finished, complete
séu buy
sêu-a clothes; shirt, blouse
sêu-a (chÓOt) dress
sì particle, often indicating a command
síp zip
sòht single, unmarried
sòng send
sôrm fork
sǒo-ay beautiful
sÒOn-la-gah-gorn customs
sòop (bOO-rèe) smoke (cigarettes) (v)
sÒOt end
sÒOt soy at the end of the soi
sǒng-klǎh Songkhla
sôrm repair
sǒrn teach
soy soi: lane
súk particle appearing before numbers
sûn short
sùng order (v)

tâh if
tâh reu-a jetty, port
tâh yung-ngún in that case
tǎhm ask (a question)
tahn eat, drink (polite)
tahng way
tahng ah-gàht by air
tahng kwǎh on the right
tahng reu-a by sea
tahng sái on the left
tài rôop take a photograph
ta-na-bùt banknote
ta-na-kahn bank
ta-nǒn street
tâo-nún only
tâo-rài? how much?
têe at
têe jum-nài dtǒo-a ticket office
têe kèe-a bOO-rèe ashtray
têe-nǎi? where?
têe-nèe here
têe-nòhn over there
têe-o visit (v)
ten-nít tennis
těung reach
toh telephone (v)
toh-ra-lâyk telegram
toh-ra-sùp telephone (n)
tǒo-ay cup
tòok correct, right

91

tòok ka-moy-ee stolen
tòok láir-o that's right!
tòok cheap
tórng sĕe-a diarrhoea
tòrt take off (clothes, shoes)
tÓO-rá business
tÔOm *denotes hours from 7 p.m. to 11 p.m.*
tum do, make
tum ngahn work (*v*)
tum-ma-dah ordinary
tum-mai? why?
tûn you (to superiors)
túng both; all
túng mòt altogether

un *general classifier*
ung-grìt English, British

wăhn sweet
wâhng free (not in use)
wâi *wai*, gesture of greeting and respect
wâi náhm swimming
way-lah time; when

wít-ta-yÓO radio
wong wee-un roundabout
wun-way one-way (traffic)
wút temple
wút prá-gâir-o Temple of the Emerald Buddha

yah medicine
yah tah ointment, cream
yah gun yOOng mosquito spray
yâhk difficult
yàhk (ja) like to, want to
yàhng née like this
yài big
yào long
yen cool; evening
yòo to be situated; to be in (at work, home)
. . . yòo têe-năi? where's . . . ?
yOOng mosquito
yÒOt stop (*v*)
yung still
yung mâi . . . not yet
yung-ngai? how?